PREPARE FOR
AN OUTPOURING OF GRACE
UPON YOUR LIFE

This self-directed, spiritual retreat has resulted in miracles in the lives and hearts of those who have applied themselves to it. St. Pope John Paul II said that his consecration to Mary was "a decisive turning point in my life." It can be the same for you.

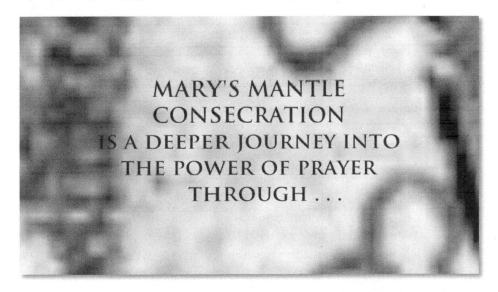

MARY'S MANTLE
CONSECRATION
IS A DEEPER JOURNEY INTO
THE POWER OF PRAYER
THROUGH . . .

MEDITATIONS ON VIRTUES AND GIFTS
THE ROSARY AND FASTING
AND YOUR CONSECRATION TO MARY

i

ENDORSEMENTS

"One of the great consolations of being Catholic is knowing that the Mother of our Lord is our Mother, too. *Mary's Mantle Consecration* deepens one's personal life of virtue, unites people in prayer, and sanctifies daily life, thus making us more like her Son and so bringing joy to her motherly heart. I am grateful to Christine Watkins for making this disarmingly simple practice, which first grew in the fertile soil of Mexican piety, available to the English-speaking world."

—Archbishop Salvatore Cordileone; San Francisco, California

"*Mary's Mantle Consecration* is a special means of responding to the call to holiness, which must be the heart and life of every disciple of Christ. I recommend it for individuals, spouses, families, and parishes as a valuable answer to the call to the New Evangelization. Our Lady of Guadalupe, the 'Star of the New Evangelization,' will assist all who seek the road to heaven."

—Bishop Myron J. Cotta; Stockton, California

"There are moments in daily life and in the Church when we feel challenged, don't know where to turn, and are searching for answers. Now more than ever we need a miracle. Christine Watkins leads us through a 46-day, self-guided retreat that focuses on daily praying of the Rosary, a little fasting, and meditating on various virtues and the seven gifts of the Holy Spirit, leading to a transformation in our lives and in the people on the journey with us! The meditations are rich with Sacred Scripture and encourage us to apply them to our current circumstances. *Mary's Mantle Consecration*, inspired by the 46 stars on Our Lady of Guadalupe's mantle, directs us to a deeper relationship of trust and dependence on our Lord for all that we need to be happy, and helps us to recognize the miracles in our lives."

—Fr. Sean O. Sheridan, TOR
President and Professor of Theology,
Franciscan University Steubenville, Ohio

"*Mary's Mantle Consecration* is a simple yet powerful way to experience the presence of God's transformative love through the tender and motherly intercession of our Mother in heaven. Christine Watkins' inspiring meditations are also practical and easily apply to anyone's daily struggles to grow in holiness, closeness to God. I wholeheartedly recommend this self-guided consecration to Mary—preparing with the Rosary, simple fasting, and the contemplation of virtues and gifts—for any intention, no matter how desperate."

—Fr. Samuel West
Pastor, St. Patrick Church, Sonora, California

"After I did Mary's Mantle Consecration, my husband stopped drinking after many years. He got on his knees, apologized to me and the kids, and started coming to Mass with us. It's just a miracle."

—Carla Agustin
Santa Rosa, California

"The meditations in *Mary's Mantle Consecration* so moved me and made such an impression on my heart that I wanted more. I knew the retreat would be the *perfect* help for the Church during this time of crisis, so I decided to coordinate one for my parish, which was made easy through daily emails. The Holy Spirit touched everyone in a special way during the 46 days, including myself—again. Many people still tell me how much they miss it and ask, 'When will we do this again?'"

—Rosanna Ruiz, wife of Deacon Mark Ruiz
St. Joseph Catholic Church; Lincoln, California

Mary's Mantle Consecration Prayer Journal
is a companion book to be used in tandem with
Mary's Mantle Consecration: A Spiritual Retreat for Heaven's Help

Available through www.QueenofPeaceMedia.com
See **www.MarysMantleConsecration.com**

Both *Mary's Mantle Consecration Prayer Journal* and
Mary's Mantle Consecration: A Spiritual Retreat for Heaven's Help
are available in Spanish/Están disponibles en español

Available through www.QueenofPeaceMedia.com
See **www.MarysMantleConsecration.com**

Weekly videos that accompany
Mary's Mantle Consecration can be ordered through
QueenofPeaceMedia.com.
Also see **www.marysmantleconsecration.com**.

The videos and book trailer are also available on the
Queen of Peace Media YouTube Channel
(http://bit.ly/2HDl65U). Click on the playlist called
MARIAN CONSECRATION SERIES
(http://bit.ly/2M3ntRg).

Children enjoy participating in the Mary's Mantle Consecration retreat by adding a daily star sticker to this beautiful, frameable, 24 x 36-inch poster of Our Lady, and coloring the downloadable pages of her image.

Available at **www.QueenofPeaceMedia/shop**.
Also see **www.MarysMantleConsecration.com**.
For bulk order discounts on all products, e-mail
orders@queenofpeacemedia.com.

Queen of Peace Media:
books, videos, blogs, prayer requests, and
more, that help you nurture your faith and
Find your way Home.

Go to **www.QueenofPeaceMedia.com**
and sign up for our newsletter to be updated
with our new content.

RADIO MARIA SHOW
"Find Something More, Find Your Way Home"
with Kendra and Christine

Tune into Christine Watkins' live weekly show with Kendra Von Esh,
Thursdays at 7 p.m. to 8 p.m., P.S.T., also posted on Queen of Peace
Media's YouTube channel. To watch or be notified of our new YouTube
videos, see http://bit.ly/2HDl65U and click "Subscribe" and the bell icon
(top right of the screen). Also go to www.queenofpeacemedia.com/home.

Visit Us on Social Media—Subscribe, Like, and Follow us!
At www.YouTube.com, search for Queen of Peace Media
Facebook: www.facebook.com/QueenofPeaceMedia
Instagram: www.instagram.com/QueenofPeaceMedia
Pinterest: www.pinterest.com/catholicvideos

ABOUT THE AUTHOR

Christine Watkins (www.ChristineWatkins.com) is an inspirational Catholic speaker and author. Her books include the Catholic best-seller,

Full of Grace: Miraculous Stories of Healing and Conversion through Mary's Intercession; and two highly acclaimed #1 Amazon best-sellers: *Of Men and Mary: How Six Men Won the Greatest Battle of Their Lives*; and *Transfigured: Patricia Sandoval's Escape from Drugs, Homelessness, and the Back Doors of Planned Parenthood*. Her latest book is *The Warning: Testimonies and Prophecies of the Illumination of Conscience*. For details, see the end of this book.

Formerly an anti-Christian atheist living a life of sin, Watkins began a life of service to the Catholic Church after a miraculous healing from Jesus through Mary, which saved her from death. Her story can be found in the book, *Full of Grace*. Before her conversion, Watkins danced professionally with the San Francisco Ballet Company. Today, she has twenty years of experience as a keynote speaker, retreat leader, spiritual director, and counselor—with ten years working as a hospice grief counselor and another ten as a post-abortion healing director. Mrs. Watkins lives in Sacramento, California with her husband and two sons.

ACKNOWLEDGMENTS

Special thanks go to Dan Osanna, Anne Manyak, William Underwood, Jamie Leatherby, and Linda Kline for sharing their keen editing eyes and golden hearts, and to Sandra Dettori for lending her notable artistic gifts to the cover.

MARY'S MANTLE CONSECRATION

A Spiritual Retreat for Heaven's Help

Christine Watkins

A Self-Guided Retreat for Busy Individuals,

Families, Groups, and Parishes

Inspired by and adapted in part from the writings of
Fr. Ignatio Larrañaga, OFM, Cap.

Imprimatur:

✠ Ramón C. Argüelles, STL
Archbishop-Emeritus of Lipa
Date: 7.28.2020

Cover background art by Sandra Lubreto Dettori. To order prints of Dettori's work, see www.etsy.com/shop/ThreeArchangels.

Books may be purchased in quantity by contacting the publisher directly at orders@queenofpeacemedia.com.

ISBN-13: 978-1-947701-06-9
ISBN-10: 1-947701-06-1

CONTENTS

CONTENTS

FOREWORD
by Monsignor James Murphy

Mary's Mantle Consecration: A Spiritual Retreat for Heaven's Help is a prayer program of consecration to the Blessed Mother that is ideally suited to life on the go.

You can do this spiritual retreat as an individual, couple, family, group, or entire congregation. And if you choose the group or congregation format, you don't have to worry about one more meeting in your life; it can be done through daily emails. *Mary's Mantle Consecration* is prayer in the electronic age!

The center of the program is the Rosary, that centuries-old prayer that has stood the test of time because it is so powerful and user-friendly. You can say the Rosary almost anywhere: while lying in bed in the dark, walking in the park, driving to work, or getting together as a family (I grew up praying it daily as a family). The important thing is that you do it in a way that suits your particular lifestyle and needs.

Fasting (not much!) is also part of the program. Don't be shocked! This is also an ancient form of prayer, and a little fasting takes on extra meaning when you do it for a personal intention: for the Church, for a family member you are worried about, or a cause you believe in. As a priest, I fast, these days, for the reparation of sin and for the healing of victims of sexual abuse, as bishops around the United States have requested. I also fast for the pope as we pass through a very difficult time in Church history.

There is also a brief daily meditation—a kind of thought for the day—based on the Theological Virtues, the Cardinal Virtues, the Seven Gifts of the Holy Spirit, and other jewels of wisdom in the Church's tradition. (Sadly, many of us can't even name the Cardinal Virtues anymore.) These meditations are excellent food for the soul, similar to the "Lectio Divina" of old. You will look forward to reading them each day.

To consecrate yourself or your family to Mary in this way, or to renew your consecration to her, is to take the matter very seriously. If the days of preparation and the final consecration are done with sincerity of heart, you are Mary's, and she is yours. I cannot think of a better way to prepare for such a consecration than by praying the very prayer Mary asks of us, the Rosary, and by contemplating and assimilating the very virtues and gifts that she possesses in full.

Available to you, as well, is *Mary's Mantle Consecration Prayer Journal*, which offers quotes from the saints, passages from Scripture, and insightful, practical questions in relation to each meditation to help the virtues and gifts come alive in your life. Don't forget to watch the accompanying weekly videos by Christine Watkins and Deacon David Leatherby, which will inspire you.

Personal prayer is at the heart of who we are as Christians, but for many of us, it gets lost in the constant noise and distraction of iPods and cell phones. The Church has given us a variety of styles and structures that help us pray more, from Charismatic groups, to the Liturgy of the Hours, to Centering Prayer, to name just a few. The problem is that these movements, good as they are, are not for everyone; some of them can be daunting for somebody who has never prayed that way before.

The strength of *Mary's Mantle Consecration* is its simplicity and familiarity. It is for all. If you are concerned about spending more time in prayer and growing in holiness, *Mary's Mantle Consecration* is a wonderful place to start.

—Msgr. James Murphy
Author of *The Martyrdom of Saint Toribio Romo*
and *Saints and Sinners in the Cristero War: Stories of Martyrdom from Mexico*

ORIGIN AND DEDICATION

There is an ancient tradition in Mexico called *"El Manto de María,"* which began in small barrios where no one was unknown and everyone had faith. In such intimate times and places of old, where news was communicated in churches, during home visits, and through town-square gossip, Mary's Mantle Consecration began.

Faithful people, poor, humble, and in love with Our Lady, would invite 46 individuals and families to participate in praying the Rosary in each other's homes. They chose 46 because that is the number of stars on the cloak, or mantle, of the supernatural image of Our Lady of Guadalupe. A woman of the barrio would sew Mary's mantle from a piece of green cloth and cut out 46 stars from gold fabric. Starting on October 28, the feast of St. Jude, those who accepted the invitation gathered at the first home in the evening, carrying the cloth mantle, the stars, and an image of Our Lady of Guadalupe. All present prayed a Rosary, and the resident family or individual attached the first gold star to Mary's green mantle. The mantle was then draped lovingly over the members of the household, who knelt before an image of Our Lady, offering their lives to her. Food and fellowship followed. On day two, the mantle traveled to the next household, where it received a second star, until the last home was visited on the 46th day, December 12, the Feast of Our Lady of Guadalupe.

Gradually, this sacred tradition was adopted by pastors throughout Mexico, who announced *"El Manto de María"* at Mass, encouraging parishioners to participate in the devotion. On the closing Feast Day of Our Lady of Guadalupe, all of the 46 families and individuals gathered in the church. Taking the green mantle, now covered with all 46 stars, they draped it ceremoniously over a statue of Our Lady and knelt before her, as words of devotion and consecration were pronounced by the priest.

The inspiration for *Mary's Mantle Consecration* came from this beautiful devotion and the fertile mind and magnanimous heart of my close friend, Patricia Sandoval—an extraordinary disciple who travels the world, sharing her unforgettable conversion story (as found in the book *Transfigured: Patricia Sandoval's Escape from Drugs, Homelessness, and the Back Doors of Planned Parenthood.*) As a bi-lingual descendent of Mexican immigrants, she learned of the *"El Manto de María"* devotion from her mother, who saw that this intimate tradition from her home country's past was being forgotten. To revive it, her mom began travelling on foot from home to home in her small Mexican neighborhood, carrying the mantle she had made by hand.

Inspired by her mother's efforts, Mrs. Sandoval reached out to 46 people whom she had met in her travels to various countries, and invited them to join *"El Manto de María."* Each day for 46 days, she sent them, electronically, a one-line description of a virtue to contemplate, and asked for their commitment of praying a daily Rosary and fasting occasionally for each other and a collective intention, thus joining her in the first "virtual" Mary's Mantle Consecration. Miracles ensued. One woman dedicated the practice to her husband who had been an abusive alcoholic for years, and as a result, he stopped drinking, apologized to his family, returned to the Catholic Church, and stayed. Many souls were healed and lives transformed. The devotion then spread to Ecuador, Colombia, and El Salvador. As Mary's mantle grew more and more resplendent, illuminated by people's daily Rosaries and days of fasting, Mary, in turn, collected more graces and showered them upon her children, in return.

Seeing that this devotion evoked such a powerful response from heaven, I wanted to offer this unique and intimate spiritual retreat in preparation for Marian consecration to a broader world. In our electronic age, with the busyness of modern life and the long roads between us, we normally cannot gather at one another's homes every night, but we can receive encouraging group emails that remind us to pray, and we can gather together in spirit with the same resulting grace. The heavenly aid gained from the 46 days of Mary's Mantle Consecration done collectively has proven to be nothing less than extraordinary.

I also wanted those who would make this consecration to have more than a short description of the virtues to contemplate each day. Help came from the life and words of a special man, a Basque Capuchin Franciscan named Fr. Ignacio Larrañaga, who died in the year 2013. The legacy of his Prayer and Life Workshops (see www.tovpil.org), which I highly recommend, inspired and shaped this book. Many of the meditations on virtues and gifts of the Holy Spirit are adapted from Fr. Larrañaga's writings, and are therefore as much his as they are my own. Help also came from St. Pope John Paul II. His prayer to Mary, which he recited in the Basilica of Our Lady of Guadalupe in Mexico in 1979 during his first foreign trip as pope, provides the sublime and timely words of consecration to Mary, bringing the devotion to a sacred close.

As a recommended bonus to the retreat, Laura Dayton and I together created the *Mary's Mantle Consecration Prayer Journal*, with thought-provoking Scripture passages, saint quotes, and carefully chosen questions. You are encouraged to use it as an individual, in prayer groups or parish congregations, in order to embrace the virtues and gifts more fully in your life—to do nothing less than become more like Mary.

In our modern age, video can provide a remarkable means of enhancing our spiritual life and knowledge, provided we choose carefully what we watch. To give you an even richer experience of the retreat, video presentations accompany this consecration with talks by myself, Christine Watkins, and Deacon David Leatherby. Children can enjoy participating by adding a daily star to a beautiful poster of Our

Lady, or coloring a page of her image. All of the above is available through www.MarysMantleConsecration.com.

I have prayed to Fr. Larrañaga and to St. Pope John Paul II, and spoken to Patricia Sandoval, asking them to join me in interceding for all who would participate in the Mary's Mantle Consecration. This book is dedicated to them: three beautiful souls who have made my life much richer—one still laboring in this life and the other two dancing freely in the next.

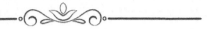

THE FOUR SPIRITUAL PRACTICES OF MARY'S MANTLE CONSECRATION

Mary's Mantle Consecration incorporates four modes of prayer that have stood the test of time and truth in moving and melting the heart of God. They are the Rosary, fasting, consecration to Mary, and through spiritual reading, striving to live the virtues and to walk in the seven gifts of the Holy Spirit.

"The goal of a virtuous life is to become like God."—St. Gregory of Nyssa

1) THE ROSARY

Participants in Mary's Mantle Consecration are invited to pray a daily Rosary—at any time of day—over the course of 46 days. There were 46 stars on the mantle of Our Lady of Guadalupe when she appeared to St. Juan Diego in 1531. These can be clearly seen today in the miraculously preserved image of Our Lady of Guadalupe in Mexico City, which is venerated by millions of pilgrims each year. The number 46 also happens to span the days of Lent from Ash Wednesday through Holy Saturday. On each of the 46 days of this retreat, a star is added to Mary's mantle. We adorn her with bright stars because she greatly appreciates our efforts and is with us in every moment of our journey to consecration.

The Holy Rosary, next to the Holy Mass, is the most powerful form of prayer there is because with each "Hail Mary," we are accompanied by the Mother of God who intercedes for us. St. Pio of Pietrelcina once commented, *"Our Lady has never refused me a grace through the recitation of the Rosary."* Pope Pius IX also said, *"Among all the devotions approved by the Church, none has been so favored by so many miracles as the devotion of the Most Holy Rosary."* In an exhortation to the universal Church, Pope Pius XI wrote, *"The Rosary is a powerful weapon to put the demons to flight and to keep oneself from sin ... If you desire peace in your hearts, in your homes, and in your country, assemble each evening to recite the Rosary. Let not even one day pass without saying it, no matter how burdened you may be with many cares and labors."*

2) FASTING

Where miracles and breakthroughs are needed, fasting is required. Fasting causes great good to happen where evil would have otherwise prevailed. When the disciples asked Jesus why they were unable to cast a demon out of a boy, Jesus responded that certain evil spirits can be overcome only through prayer and fasting. Such are the demons that confront our world and the Church at this time. (Translations of the Gospel of Mark 9:29, such as the *Revised Standard Version Catholic Edition*, say: *"And he said to them, 'This kind cannot be driven out by anything but prayer and fasting.'"*)

Fasting for, at minimum, one day is an important component of the retreat. The suggested fast is bread and water. (For those with health limitations, a modified fast can be observed. This might mean cutting out desserts and coffee, or eating only vegetables, beans and/or nuts, and drinking plenty of water.)

Biblical accounts of fasting always refer to the simplification or absence of food. Jesus fasted from food and water for 40 days and nights, and He assumes that all of His disciples are fasting. In the Gospel of Matthew, He says, *"When you fast, do not look gloomy like the hypocrites"* (6:16a). Biblical fasting ushers in windfalls of grace and precedes great things. Moses fasted for 40 days before receiving the Ten Commandments (Exodus 34:28). Queen Esther invoked a fast to save the Jews of the Persian Empire from extermination (Esther 4:16). At the call of the prophet Jonah, the Ninevites fasted and their lives were spared (Jonah 3:5-9). The first disciples fasted for their election and commissioning of Christian leaders (Acts 13:3-4, 14:23). And after His sojourn of fasting in the desert, Jesus's public ministry began.

The spiritual practice of fasting from food reaches into the core of our being, giving us more life in the Spirit and less in the "flesh," thus transforming who we are. Bad habits can be removed by their roots, not simply their branches. Cravings for the things of this world can vanish, as our will comes more under our control.

Fasting can also offer clear answers to problems, cure addictions, prevent famine and wars, and suspend natural laws. According to St. Basil the Great:

> *Fasting gives birth to prophets and strengthens the powerful; fasting makes lawgivers wise. Fasting is a good safeguard for the soul, a steadfast companion for the body, a weapon for the valiant, and a gymnasium for athletes. Fasting repels temptations, anoints unto piety; it is the comrade of watchfulness and the artificer of chastity. In war it fights bravely, in peace it teaches stillness.*

3) CONTEMPLATION OF VIRTUES AND THE SEVEN GIFTS OF THE HOLY SPIRIT

Mary's Mantle Consecration invites participants to read the daily meditations in this book, which highlight aspects of a virtue or a gift of the Holy Spirit. This spiritual reading takes only a couple minutes and can be done at any time of day. The companion book, *Mary's Mantle Consecration Prayer Journal,* is a helpful aid to incorporate more profoundly these virtues or gifts into your daily life.

Mary possessed in her soul every virtue and the seven gifts of the Holy Spirit to their fullest human extent. By meditating upon these same virtues and gifts, and striving to incorporate them more fully into our own souls, we become more like Mary. Thus we prepare ourselves well for a true and intimate consecration to the Mother of God.

Prayers that emanate from a pure and virtuous heart are most pleasing to God and incline His ear in a direct way. We become more effective prayer warriors when we cultivate the virtues and open ourselves to the seven gifts of the Holy Spirit: wisdom, understanding, counsel, fortitude, knowledge, piety, and fear or awe of the Lord. Scripture attests to the power of a righteous person's prayer:

> *Therefore, confess your sins to one another and pray for one another, that you may be healed. The fervent prayer of a righteous person is very powerful. Elijah was a human being like us; yet he prayed earnestly that it might not rain, and for three years and six months it did not rain upon the land. Then he prayed again, and the sky gave rain and the earth produced its fruit.* (James 5:16-18)

If you remain in me and my words remain in you, ask for whatever you want and it will be done for you. By this is my Father glorified, that you bear much fruit and become my disciples. (John 15:7-8)

Beloved, if [our] hearts do not condemn us, we have confidence in God and receive from him whatever we ask, because we keep his commandments and do what pleases him. (1 John 3:21-22)

4) CONSECRATION TO MARY

The end goal of *Mary's Mantle Consecration* is the same as that of every authentic Marian consecration: perfect union with Jesus Christ through a total gift of all that we are, and the offering of ourselves to Our Lady. When we consecrate ourselves to Mary, we give her our bodies, our souls, and the value of our good works and prayers—past, present, and future—to use and distribute as she wills. She is the Mediatrix of All Graces, which means that all of God's graces are distributed to the world through her. Thus Mary, in return for our consecration, uses the full power of her intercession to help conform us to Christ. To be an open vessel to receive the fullness of grace that God and Mary wish to impart to us, it is important that we receive the Sacrament of Reconciliation within a few days leading up to the final consecration.

No one is ever forced to consecrate himself or herself to Our Lady, but we are all called by God to holiness of life, to be saints. We can choose Option A, to strive for sainthood without Mary's full assistance; or Option B, to become like Christ with the full force of the prayers of the Mediatrix of All Graces. To be consecrated to Mary is a great gift from heaven. That is why popes and saints and mystics have long invited us to make a formal consecration to her.

Marian consecration began in the 4th and 5th centuries. Early African sermons from this period speak of becoming voluntary "slaves of Mary." By the 8th century, people like St. John Damascene in the east (d. 749) were authoring prayers of consecration to the Mother of God: *"O Lady, before you we take our stand. Lady, I call you Virgin Mother of God. And to your hope, as to the surest and strongest anchor, we bind ourselves to you."*

In the 17th century, St. Louis-Marie de Montfort (1673-1716) became the champion of Marian consecration through his seminal work, *True Devotion to Mary,* which was discovered after his death. In this spiritual classic, he describes total consecration to Mary as "the surest, easiest, and most perfect means" to becoming a saint. St. Pope John Paul II adopted as his personal motto, *"Totus Tuus,"* the words that begin St. Louis-Marie de Montfort's Marian consecration:

"Totus tuus ego sum, et omnia mea tua sunt, O Virgo, super omnia benedicta."

"I am all yours, and all that is mine is yours, O Virgin, blessed above all."

While modern scholars hold that St. Louis-Marie de Montfort's consecration was to Jesus through Mary, it was addressed directly to Mary, as were the first texts of Marian consecration in the Church. We need not worry that by giving all that we are to Mary, we will lose sight of Jesus, Our Savior. For as St. Louis-Marie de Montfort also says, "The more a soul is consecrated to Mary, the more it is consecrated to Jesus Christ" (*True Devotion to Mary,* Section 120).

Nor should we fear that by giving to Mary our very selves and the merits of our prayers and good works, that our needs or those of our loved ones will be forgotten. Mary, who is intimately aware of the state of the Church and of the entire world at any given moment, uses our offering for the greatest possible salvation of souls—and at the same time, perfectly and remarkably, for our own personal salvation and sanctification. Our extremely limited human awareness cannot compare to the extraordinary ability to know the spiritual state and needs of seven billion souls. This is the vantage point of the Mother of God.

Taking perfect care of us, Mary will first distribute our merits toward our personal vocation in life, and do so in the best possible way. She will lead us to fulfill our obligations to our given state and calling. Moreover, Mary flawlessly dispenses the graces we merit even when we forget, or have no way of discerning, who most needs our prayers and sacrifices. Our Mother knows best.

St. Louis-Marie de Montfort also assured us that it is always meritorious to give away merit. We will receive exponentially more than what we offer of ourselves in our act of consecration. To say this in the simplest of terms, we help Our Lady take care of the world, and she takes care of our souls and those of our loved ones better than we ever could.

11

HOW TO PARTICIPATE IN MARY'S MANTLE CONSECRATION

The 46-day preparation of *Mary's Mantle Consecration* can be done by individuals, couples, families, groups, or entire congregations. Please note: Mary's Mantle Consecration does not have to be done perfectly. God rejoices in our trying. If you miss a day of prayer or stumble in your attempts, allow God's mercy and appreciation for your efforts to enfold you, leaving no room for discouragement or self-reproach. If you desire, you may use *Mary's Mantle Consecration Prayer Journal* to complement and deepen your preparation for consecration.

This consecration to Mary should end, ideally, on a Marian Feast Day, or if done as part of your Lenten journey, on Holy Saturday. In the Roman Catholic Church, the consecration schedule is as follows for the United States:

Starting Date	Marian Feast Day	Consecration Date
Ash Wednesday	Holy Saturday (not a Marian Feast Day)	Holy Saturday
February 8	Annunciation	March 25
March 29	Our Lady of Fatima	May 13
April 16	Visitation	May 31
May 13	Our Mother of Perpetual Help	June 27
June 1	Our Lady of Mount Carmel	July 16
July 1	Assumption*	August 15
July 8	Queenship of Mary	August 22
July 12	Our Lady of Czestochowa	August 26
July 25	Birth of Mary	September 8
July 29	The Most Holy Name of Mary	September 12
August 1	Our Lady of Sorrows	September 15
August 23	Our Lady of the Rosary	October 7
October 7	Presentation of the Blessed Virgin Mary	November 21
October 24	Immaculate Conception*	December 8
October 28	Our Lady of Guadalupe	December 12

November 17	Solemnity of Mary, Mother of God*	January 1
November 24	Our Lady of Prompt Succor	January 8
December 19	Presentation of the Lord	February 2
December 28	Our Lady of Lourdes	February 11
Note: The Feast of the Blessed Virgin Mary, Mother of the Church, is the Monday after Pentecost. The Feast of the Immaculate Heart is the Saturday following the second Sunday after Pentecost.		

*Holy Day of Obligation

Marian Feast Days are holy days of the liturgical year, celebrated because of their local, regional, national, or international importance. Some feasts celebrate certain events in the life of Mary, while others recognize Mary's ongoing involvement in the life of the Church. There are hundreds of Marian Feast Days from around the world that may conclude the consecration, such as Our Lady of Africa (April 30), Our Lady of Czestochowa (August 26), Our Lady of La Vang (November 22), or Our Lady of Walsingham, England (September 24). For a comprehensive list of feast days, see www.MarysMantle Consecration.com.

Videos for Mary's Mantle Consecration

The weekly Marian Consecration Series videos by Christine Watkins and Deacon David Leatherby are an added plus for this unique consecration. The first two videos should be viewed before the retreat begins, and the others should be watched weekly, on any given day. The final video (Part 7) should be viewed before your final consecration day.

VIDEO	MARIAN CONSECRATION SERIES
Before the retreat begins	Why People Are Raving about Mary's Mantle Consecration: Amazing Parishioner Testimonies
Before the retreat begins	Introduction to a Most Powerful Consecration to Mary That Changes Lives: Mary's Mantle Consecration
Part 1, retreat week 1	What Does Consecration to Mary Mean?
Part 2, retreat week 2	Why the Rosary Has Such Power and How to Pray It Effectively
Part 3, retreat week 3	The Untapped Power of Fasting to Change Our Lives and Loved Ones

Part 4, retreat week 4	Why Extraordinary Virtue Is Needed in Our Difficult Times
Part 5, retreat week 5	What You Don't Know but Need to Know About Confession and Joy
Part 6, retreat week 6	Why Are Virtues So Hard and Vices So Easy?
Part 7, week 7 before the final consecration date	Why Mary Is the Model of Discipleship and How She Can Help You

The Marian Consecration Video Series is available on DVD through www.MarysMantleConsecration.com or on the Queen of Peace Media YouTube channel at http://bit.ly/2M3ntRg.

HOW CHILDREN CAN PARTICIPATE

Due to a demand from mothers, Mary's Mantle Consecration offers a stunning 24 x 36-inch poster of Our Lady, which comes with star stickers. Each day of the retreat, children can enjoy adding a sticker to Mary's mantle, filling it with stars. Each star signifies the offering of their love and prayers for that day. Adults are encouraged to explain to the child(ren) that Our Lady sees them, loves them, knows them, and thanks them each time that they adorn her mantle. Their offering is just as real for her as it is for them. Many choose to frame the poster, hanging it on their wall as a reminder of their consecration to the Mother of God and her maternal protection and care for them.

Also available for children of all ages (and for adults who enjoy coloring) is a downloadable coloring page of Our Lady. The poster and page can be found at www.MarysMantleConsecration.com. For free shipping on bulk orders, email orders@queenofpeacemedia.com.

After the consecration has ended, please consider sending any testimonies of the fruits received to cwatkins@queenofpeacemedia.com. Thank you, in advance, for your efforts on behalf of the Kingdom. May you always find refuge under the mantle of Mother Mary, who loves you as her own.

1. Done as an individual

Individuals pray a daily Rosary, read a daily meditation contained in this book, watch the videos, and fast every Wednesday or Friday (traditional fasting days in the Church) over the course of the 46 days. The suggested fast is bread and water. If health reasons prevent this, one may fast on other simple, bland foods such as raw vegetables and nuts. The focus of the prayer and the sacrifice of the fasting is for a particular intention, or intentions, dear to one's heart. The Rosary and spiritual reading can be done in any order or time of day, and the goal of the reading is to practice that day's virtue, or to welcome that day's gift of the Holy Spirit.

2. Done as a couple or family

With personal and/or collective intentions in mind, the participants pray a daily Rosary for 46 days, read a meditation each day (aloud and together, when possible), watch the weekly videos, and try to incorporate the day's virtue or gift into everyday life. The order and time that either the Rosary or reading occurs depends upon one's schedule.

Each week, one or more of the members fast on a Wednesday or Friday. The schedule of who fasts on what week is arranged by the couple or family. For adults, the suggested fast is bread and water. If health reasons prevent this, adults may fast on other simple, bland foods such as raw vegetables and nuts. Children can fast by having soup for dinner, offering up dessert, eating toast without jelly or butter, etc. Encourage children by assuring them that when they make these smaller sacrifices, they are doing something very beautiful and powerful for God.

It is unifying if couples can say a full Rosary together, but sometimes schedules and situations may not permit this. In such cases, the Rosary can be said separately or by only one of the spouses. Adults are encouraged to read the Scripture and saint quotes and journal each day in *Mary's Mantle Consecration Prayer Journal*. Children who are not accustomed to saying a full Rosary every day can participate in a decade or two and listen to their parent(s) or caregiver(s) say the rest, but not be forced to. Children enjoy coloring the Mary's Mantle picture page and/or adding a daily star sticker to Our Lady's mantle on the beautiful Mary's Mantle poster. See "How Children Can Participate" above.

3. DONE AS A GROUP OR PARISH

In addition to the information below, please see the detailed instructions and check list for the group or parish leader at www.MarysMantleConsecration.com. Click on "Group or Parish Coordinator Instructions."

Mary's Mantle Consecration done as a group or in a parish provides an inspiring and organized means to consecrate large numbers of the faithful to Mary, and to collectively intercede for a particular intention. Conflicts and differences in groups and parishes can dissolve, evils within communities can be eradicated, and the Catholic Church can experience healing and unification through the unparalleled power of communal prayer and fasting.

Ending the consecration on a Feast Day of Our Lady is ideal. Some groups or parishes choose to begin the program on October 28 and end on the Feast of Our Lady of Guadalupe, December 12. Others choose a Feast Day of special importance to their parish. The 46-day program is particularly suitable for a collective Lenten observance because there are 46 days from Ash Wednesday through Holy Saturday. The coordinator may wish to organize a physical get-together for the weekly video talks followed by group discussion questions, which are at the end of each DVD of the Marian Consecration Series, as well as available online: click on "Video Discussion Questions" online at www.MarysMantleConsecration.com. A coordinator may also choose to gather people for the last day of the retreat, when the final consecration prayer is recited and the consecration certificates are signed.

To begin, a coordinator is assigned and gathers, with helpers, anywhere from seven to a couple of hundred people. In this format, the coordinator sends out daily e-mails to the participants and ensures that they obtain a copy of this book, and the optional *Mary's Mantle Consecration Prayer Journal*. Participants may also wish to order the Mary's Mantle coloring page and/or the beautiful Mary's Mantle poster on which children can add a star sticker daily to Our Lady's mantle, available at www.MarysMantleConsecration.com. (For discounted bulk orders of the books and posters, e-mail Queen of Peace Media at orders@queenofpeacemedia.com.)

Retreat participants are called "Stars" and offer up their prayers and fasting for all of the participants, their loved ones, and the group's collective intention. The daily e-mails remind participants of the prayer intention; the daily virtue or gift to read about and meditate upon; which person, or Star, is assigned to fast that day; and which Star will fast the following day. On each participant's fasting day, the entire group will remember that person in their Rosary prayers.

Doing Mary's Mantle Consecration in this format provides an intimate experience for the participants. Each person becomes a Star on Our Lady's mantle as he or she is prayed for by name by the entire group.

In his book, *The Secret of the Rosary*, St. Louis-Marie de Montfort wrote: "*Somebody who says his Rosary alone only gains the merit of one Rosary, but if he says it together with thirty other people, he gains the merit of thirty Rosaries … 'In union there is strength.'*" When the preparation for consecration is done in this way, imagine the joy it brings to Mary and the glory it gives to God. In a group with 46 people participating, each person receives the merits of 2,116 Rosaries and 46 days of fasting. This spiritual multiplier effect will be even greater for larger groups. Miracles will surely happen!

At the beginning of the 46 days of prayer and fasting, no stars will be illuminated on Mary's mantle. By the end, her mantle will shine brightly, thanks to all who participate!

DAY 1:   DAY 46:

A Prayer to Begin

O most Holy Mother, whom I love tenderly as my own, in your sacred presence, I offer to you these days of preparation for consecration in honor of the stars that adorned your heavenly mantle. I appeal to you to intercede these 46 days for all of my needs, for those of my loved ones, and for [your intention(s)]. Please show me the sweet compassion that you showered upon St. Juan Diego, your messenger. Please give me a pure and virtuous heart, like your own, so that I might derive the same consolation—the soothing of my pains and the lifting of my soul—that

18

Juan Diego received from the gentle words you gave to him centuries ago:

"Listen, put it into your heart, my dearest one, that the thing that disturbs you, the thing that afflicts you, is nothing. Do not let your countenance, your heart be disturbed. Do not fear any sickness, nor anything that is sharp or hurtful. Am I not here, I, who am your Mother? Are you not under my shadow and protection? Am I not the source of your joy? Are you not in the hollow of my mantle, in the crossing of my arms? Do you need anything more?"

Let Us Adorn
Mary's Mantle with Stars

MEDITATIONS ON VIRTUES

AND THE SEVEN

GIFTS OF THE HOLY SPIRIT

1st Star

THANKSGIVING

Let us begin this Mary's Mantle consecration preparation with prayer:

Mold my heart, Lord Jesus, and awaken my soul to the dreams of mankind from the beginning of time. In Your eyes shine the hopes of centuries, the laughter of small children, and the brilliance of galaxies.

Renew in me, Holy Spirit, the forces of divine winds. You Who color the world with beauty, dazzle the eye with wonder, and dance through every lullaby, breathe in me.

Father of tenderness, make my voice a note in your symphony, my movements a part of your dance, my thoughts a blueprint of Your mind.

Holy Trinity, fill me with Your insatiable desire to capture souls. Take me to Your lost and Your poor, and with outstretched arms and conforming tears, exchange my heart for Yours.

Expanding fire, incomprehensible light and joy beyond ecstasy, my whole being is filled with thanksgiving—for You brought me into life from a single thought of love. You created me, so small and insignificant, to give me heights above the angels. I came from nothing and offered You so little; yet Your reward for me is a place beyond dreams, a luminous dwelling in a land of unending peace.

2nd Star

COMMITMENT

Try. This one word encapsulates all that God asks of us. Just try. God is well aware of our limitations, our insecurities, our personality flaws. He knows. There is no need for us to hide. To try to somehow shelter God from the truth of who we are is folly and madness; rather, we must expose all of ourselves to the Lord and love Him as we are. If we wait until we are beacons of perfection to love Him, we never will. Holiness is not forged from the habit of throwing our flaws into a dark closet or hastily shoving them under the bed before kneeling to pray. It arises from the labor of continually exposing our weaknesses in contemplation and Confession, where darkness vanishes into light and ugliness fades into beauty.

Arise each morning and go in search of the Face of the Lord, even if His cheek seems to vanish in the moment you reach to touch it. Try. We are all bottomless wells, made in the image, measure, and likeness of God. An infinite number of finites will never satisfy us; only what is infinite can fill to overflowing a well that runs so deep. Yet we are paradoxical beings, always running after other creatures and things of this world, whose measures do not correspond to ours. For that reason, we are restless and dissatisfied. Without realizing it, we are seeking water in desert landscapes and chasing shadows in search of eternal light.

Arise each morning and commit to holiness, the only journey worth traveling. In every endeavor, in every moment, seek to imitate the Lord. Try.

God sees and applauds us when we pick up our crosses and conquer our weaknesses, and He catches us when we fall trying. He sees that we wanted to love Him, but our wretched flesh didn't allow us to fully express our love. Gather your shattered crosses and try again. That is all He asks. It is when we are trying to love Him that we shine in heaven's eyes. It is when we are trying to love Him that He turns our frailty into strength. It is when we are trying to love Him that He stands close by our side, offering His shoulder to lean on.

We can only fail if we fail to try.

3rd Star

LOVE

(one of the three Theological Virtues)

Where there is love, there is God, for God *is* Love. But this word "love" is so often grossly misunderstood, so misused and misappropriated. For a great deal of the time, when we believe we love, in reality, we are pleasing ourselves.

I could dedicate myself tirelessly to fighting for a just cause, and surely those I free from oppression will say: "This person loves us all so much!" I may donate a substantial sum of money, but what if I am not thanked? My motives, conscious or not, might be to gain power, popularity, a good name, to be appreciated or a hero in someone's eyes. Whom or what did I love? Did I serve the people or myself?

I say I love my friend. But if I hear one day that she betrayed my confidence, and I vow, "She is no longer any friend of mine!" I have, in effect, slammed forever shut the doors of love and trust. Who loved whom? Did I truly love my friend, or did I love myself in her? How could I love her one day and not the next? Is that how Jesus loves her?

Everything depends on our intentions. The same work I carry out with selfless charity could also be performed to satisfy narcissism and greed. This may happen without others or perhaps even myself recognizing the difference.

True love is tested on the cross. God's love for us is the greatest power there is, a force infinitely more formidable than any on earth, and nowhere was God's love more manifest than when He hung helplessly on the Cross. If we do not love the cross, our love for God and others is shallow, perhaps even self-indulgent. So often this is all that human love is.

Love requires sacrifice, and love of Jesus and our neighbor costs a great deal. We don't often realize that we will not be happy until we learn to embrace and love the cross. This is what Jesus did, and what He asks us to do. The cross is hard and cold, like the world; but we can make ourselves soft and warm by carrying it. We are called to love God and others down to the last letter of God's will, even if it means giving our life for Him.

Selflessly we must approach our lives. Selflessly we must approach the world. And in selfless love, we will taste eternal life.

4th Star

TRUST

"*Do not worry*"..."*Do not fear*" is the message God speaks to us through His Word more than any other.

The One who made us has in mind a plan. In each soul lives a vocation, whether asleep in distraction and disbelief, or awake and pulsating in purpose and force. Could God expect us to do His will while He hides the way? No! Always, in the mystery of His timing, He reveals to us the next step . . . and the next, through subtle promptings and gentle nudges, if not resounding shouts. A heart attuned to Him knows this. "*My sheep hear my voice; I know them, and they follow me*" (John 10:27). It is not our calling or duty to plan our lives down to the last controlling detail—a task that can be filled with presumption and pride. Our job is to pray and to follow the next footprint God leaves for us.

For now, there is only one thing that is needed: to love God with all that we have, and to love others as ourselves. If our day is spent in turmoil over tomorrow, our Father's will has vanished in the clouds of worry. Did our eyes rise to see the man sitting on the train? He was desperate for a kind hello. Did our ears hear the Spirit prompting us to speak to our co-worker? She needed fraternal correction. Did we notice the girl sitting on the sidewalk? She was hungry for God's Word because no one had ever fed her. Or were we so lost in our anxious thoughts over God's plan for our lives that we neglected to follow just that?

How God suffers when He sees us so agitated and upset! How He tries to reassure us when we listen to our fears. Even after extending our cares to Him, we can pull matters back into our grasp, like a child who claims impertinently that she can do the cooking better than her mother and then takes over the kitchen, causing an ungodly mess.

Our worry literally binds God's hands. But every act of complete, blind trust unties them, causing the best effect possible, for God can accomplish what no human being is capable of. It is when we truly release our worries to the Lord and rest our head on His lap in peace, that He can work for us the most glorious of miracles.

5th Star

KINDNESS

Jesus Christ, my Lord and brother, make me kind. Pour into me a spirit so courteous that I may give to others the same consideration I would have for You.

Place a bolt on the door of my heart so that I may not think evil of anyone, judge unfavorably, misinterpret events, or make wrong assumptions. Quiet my mind should I begin to invade the sacred sanctuary of intentions.

When the temptation to speak ill of a brother or sister rises into my throat, seal my lips with silence so that I may never spill gossip or break promises. May I keep confidences until death. May my presence heal, my tongue encourage, and my actions soothe the aches of human hearts. May I leave behind me a trail of blessings wherever You would have me go.

6th Star

TENACITY

When we lose our tenacious hold of a private life with the Lord, God feels more distant. No longer the cause for emotion, He becomes an abstraction—a word that carries less and less meaning. He is no longer that special Someone.

No one brims with sustained excitement over improving themselves for a theory; no one fancies dancing with a stale conjecture. As prayer declines, so does one's source of true joy, and when there is little to no perceived benefit and satisfaction in prayer, there is less of a desire to be with God.

At its principle and foundation, the center of Christian life is God. So when God ceases to be the center of gravity, and prayer is no longer the fulcrum of one's life, the "I" rises up with all of its egotistical demands, leaving the soul fragile, impatient, rigid, sinful, and irritable. The only Someone who can control these implacable demands has been abandoned, and we inevitably descend along a spiral of disenchantment. When prayer is abandoned, great voids open up automatically everywhere, and based on the law of displacement, compensations of kinds set up camp. God tries, but can no longer awaken joy in our hearts for there is no room left for Him.

Many have been predisposed with a sensitivity to the divine so keen, a mystical capacity so extraordinary, that if they had diligently cultivated it, today they would be stars of the first magnitude in the Church. Meanwhile, they vegetate in mediocrity and dissatisfaction, not because grace has failed them, but because they have not held on tenaciously to God. Through an ordered and regular practice of prayer—even amidst thunderous temptations, harsh aridity, inconvenience, and innumerable fears—spiritual seeds could have sprouted and grown. But instead of becoming lush and sturdy trees, standing fifty feet tall, covering many others with shelter and shade, these people remain brittle bushes only four feet high. Imagine their profound discontent.

When a Christian ceases to pray, God vanishes, not in and of Himself, but in that person. For a Christian, and more so for a militant disciple, tenacity in prayer is a matter of life or death.

7th Star

ENDURANCE

A prayer in depression and loneliness. . .

Lord, I feel so sad, and I miss times long gone. The dark night has descended and obscured Your light. My insides are twisted into thorny vines. Confusion is my daily bread. I search for a true friend and reach for dreams, while my spirit languishes in forced conversation and banal distractions. I am alone.

My mightiest of efforts lead nowhere, and my hands reach out to touch failure. My family is a home of strangers, our unity broken into factions of silence and scorn. Where is your Good News? Is there none for me? When I cling to You, I cannot feel You. When I talk with You, I cannot hear You. You say You are there, but You are as elusive as a sunrise at midnight or a bonfire in a frozen tundra.

Do not take away Your hand from me, Father. Do not close Your ears to my silent screams at night. How can You be my light when I cannot see You? How can You be my rock when I cannot feel You under my feet? The ground below is trembling and cracking, and the sky above is closing off the stars. Where did You go? The darkness, it scares me, and I need You. Give me at least one sign, one scant hint, that You care, that You exist.

You once felt so close as to fill my lungs with Your breath, but now I feel dropped, like a ball with no air. Yet even in this journey of frightening sadness and meaningless hours, I will take one step forward, and tomorrow another. I will endure because my desolation is not truth and the shadows speak lies. Beyond my shattered mind is a beautiful life and a beautiful me that I cannot see. But You do, my Lord. You do.

8th Star

FORGIVENESS

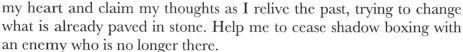

It happens seldom that someone seeks to offend me. It happens often that I feel offended. When I remain indignant, who suffers, Lord? Is it the one whom I dislike, or is it I, the one who is disliking? My bitterness is eating at me, destroying me like a cancer, while my perceived enemy sleeps peacefully unaware.

Sharp resentments puncture my heart and claim my thoughts as I relive the past, trying to change what is already paved in stone. Help me to cease shadow boxing with an enemy who is no longer there.

I am suffering needlessly. Please help me, Lord, to stop flinging mental stones of ill will, day and night. My wounds are deep and I cannot end this insanity without You. To stir up and feed rancor, I know, is madness. Is there any fatigue so unsettling as the one produced by resentment? Is there is any release so sweet as the restful sigh of forgiveness?

Please forgive all my trespasses, as I forgive those who trespass against me.

An exercise in forgiveness: adopting the heart of Jesus

Sitting quietly and still, place yourself in the inner world of Jesus. Identify with His entire being, in such a way that His Spirit lives in yours. Your thoughts become His thoughts; your eyes become His eyes; your heart, His heart.

Now place your enemy(ies) in your mind's eye before you, and try to see them through the eyes of Christ. Feel toward them what Jesus feels; reach out to embrace them as Jesus would. Encircle them with the arms of the Lord, as if there were no separation between you and the movements of God. In sacred intimacy, as if you and Jesus were a single being, forgive, understand, and hold your enemy in your arms for a long time until you feel a great peace.

9ᵗʰ Star

PERSEVERANCE

Persevere, my friend, persevere.

Continue believing in goodness, ultimate goodness, when evil has had its day.

Continue to lower your bucket into the well of prayer, even though you haven't drawn a drop.

Continue to rise each morning, though your limbs should refuse to move.

Continue to search for meaning in unavoidable suffering, when nothing makes sense.

Continue to cast your line into the sea of lost souls, though not one fish takes a bite.

Continue to perform your duties, even if drudgery should dampen your spirit.

Continue to work beyond failures, disappointments, and detours, pressing toward the Goal.

Persevere, my friend, persevere, for the dark night is ending, dawn is breaking on the horizon, and the sun will soon rise.

10th Star

ACCEPTANCE

The human being, without having tried or wished for it, finds herself on earth. She did not choose her parents. She did not choose her hometown or her looks. Those realities that she never wanted or never chose can become anathema. In frustration, she releases emotional aggression in order to attack and destroy them in her mind.

A person can come to live in a perpetual battle against all that displeases her. Ashamed and saddened, she rejects herself and her circumstances: her weight, her nose, her temperament, her commute, her moodiness, her acquaintances, her political enemies, her relatives, mosquitoes, and withering heat . . . She resists everything that she dislikes but cannot change, and she labels it her adversary. As a result, she becomes depressed, anxious, and suspicious.

If I abhor my reflection in the mirror, it is my enemy. If I reject the shrill voice of my neighbor, it is my enemy. My adversaries, therefore, live within me to the extent that I give them life through my resistance.

Yet within me are also friends. The first stage of inner freedom involves befriending myself. If I accept my aging eyes or my awkward gait, they become my friends. The problem is not with my slowness in math or inability to deliver a good punchline, but in my rejection of my deficits and failures. No matter how unlikeable another may be, if I embrace him, he is my friend. In acceptance, this ill-timed storm becomes brother storm; this influenza virus becomes sister flu. And if I accept my life's end, I have befriended death. Thus, no matter who I am or the circumstances of my existence, I can choose to live in the crossfire of a battle zone of my own making, or within the boundaries of a peaceful, temperate forest.

The power lies within me to embrace or reject those things I cannot change; thus the alchemy to turn evil into good rests in the palm of my hands.

11th Star

PATIENCE

Patience begins with knowing and accepting peacefully that we are essentially limited. We desire to do and be something great; but in this life, we are able to do little, and the little we will do with great effort will yield limited results. Herein lies true wisdom and humility, if we can accept our limited nature. Even the great saints didn't know of their own greatness and wished they had been able to do and be so much more.

Illusion leads to disillusion. Staring at the stars, pondering the universe, contemplating the infinite accomplishments and attributes of the Almighty, how can we feel anything but small? In reality, we fly very low in comparison with the divine heights of Jesus.

Be saddened by our state? No. Ashamed of who we are? Never. The peaceful key to weathering the slow progression of holiness in ourselves and others, and accepting the timing of God in the world—is patience.

A woman planted an extensive field of wheat. She returned the next week and saw that nothing had sprouted. It seemed to her that the seeds had died in the coffin-like soil. Disappointed, she came back two weeks later only to find that everything looked the same: no signs of life. Then four weeks passed, and she delighted to see, as she walked into the field, that tender green shoots had poked timidly up from the earth. Time journeyed on and inches of winter snow piled itself on top of the fledgling stalks, flattening them under its weight. But the wheat plants persevered.

Then a terrible frost came, relentless in its threat to destroy. The wheat could not grow and lost many of its blades, but still clung obstinately to life. Spring finally arrived and the wheat began to breathe. In time, brave stalks began to reach upward for the sun. But from one month to the next, their growth was so slow that the woman could not see any change. A few months went by, and she returned. Much to her joy and surprise, extending before her and over the horizon was an immense and majestic golden wheat field, swaying and undulating in the breeze.

Whether as the wheat or the woman, one can put forth all the impatient fretting in the world and not make the wheat grow one day sooner or one inch taller. Patience achieves all.

12th Star

HUMILITY

When I feel the desire for others to speak well of me, I will remember how Jesus shunned all praise and fame when He cured the sick and multiplied the loaves. I will remind myself of how His mother, the most exalted and exquisite of all human beings, lived her days in quiet love, without fanfare, never calling attention to herself.

When I desire wealth and ease, I will think of the Lord's challenge: "*Foxes have dens and birds of the sky have nests, but the Son of Man has nowhere to rest his head*" (Luke 9:58). I will tame myself with His warning: "*But woe to you who are rich, for you have received your consolation*" (Luke 6:24).

When I seek to satisfy my appetite for materialism and comfort, I will reflect on the daily life of Mary, a poor and humble woman from an underdeveloped nation, who had to fetch and carry water in a heavy bucket, cut and break branches for firewood, tend to goats and chickens, and grind wheat with stones. The Queen of Heaven and Earth had no central heating, no air conditioning, no aspirin for a headache. Her queenship was without soft, delicate hands and personal servants.

When I realize that I am spending my precious time looking out for myself, I will recall that Jesus never acted in this way. He lived his life solely for others, renouncing His advantages of being God, submitting Himself to the life of a poor carpenter and an itinerant, and eventually to a violent, untimely death. When I think nothing of putting myself first, I will turn my thoughts to Mary, who was quick in mind and body to help those in need: . . . *Mary set out and traveled to the hill country in haste to a town of Judah, where she entered the house of Zechariah and greeted Elizabeth* (Luke 1:23-39-40). *When the wine ran short, the mother of Jesus said to him, "They have no wine"* (John 2:3).

When I focus my talents around my own goals and desires and refuse to ask God what His will for my life is, I will bring to mind Mary's fiat, which began with the Annunciation and had no greater expression than her quiet presence at the Crucifixion: *"I am the handmaiden of the Lord, let it be done to me according to thy word."* And I will say, like Jesus in the Garden of Olives, *". . . not my will but Yours be done"* (Luke 22:42).

When my pride roars within me, insisting that my ego be fed and my will satisfied, I will remember that I am only truly great when I am most humble.

13ᵗʰ Star

KNOWLEDGE

(one of the Seven Gifts of the Holy Spirit)

It is one thing to speak of a snow bank; but to fall headlong into one is another experience altogether. It is one thing to take a picture of a mom staring lovingly into the eyes of her child; it is quite another to see through the eyes of that mother. To have the mental concept of a fever is not to suffer through one. To learn why birds fly is not the same as soaring through the air with expansive wings. To simply read Holy Scripture is not to know it in one's heart.

God, too, is not a concept, theory, or theology. He is a Person, a Person who can be known and followed through an experiential relationship. Facts and verses, stored and memorized, do not a prophet make. A catechized person may express articles of faith articulately, even poetically; but a prophetic witness is also fashioned from solitary, prolonged encounters, face to face, with the Lord. The greatest friends of Jesus are forged on their knees, daily, in intense prayer. These are the ones who see the whole spectrum of creative things insofar as they lead us to God, who can discern life through the eyes of the supernatural. These are the disciples that the Church needs and desires.

I ask you, Lord, now, to help me to be one of Your true prophets. Help me forever seek Your presence and intimate embrace. If I do not, I will never know You.

14ᵗʰ Star

MEEKNESS

"*Take my yoke upon you and learn from me, for I am meek and humble of heart; and you will find rest for yourselves*" (Matthew 11:29). Meekness is a virtue that Jesus alone inculcated, and which no ancient philosopher seems to have understood or recommended. Even our modern usage of "meek" can be dominated by a sense of weakness, cowardice, or people-pleasing. In Jesus' mouth, it is not that. To be meek is to be a spiritual rock. In the evangelical sense, meekness is humility, resignation, submission to the Divine Will without murmuring or peevishness. It is mildness of temper, softness in dealing with others, and forbearance under difficulties, setbacks, and injuries. One who is meek is not easily provoked or irritated.

By reason of being born into the world, we naturally create an illusion in our minds of who we are, a treasured lie for which we long, fight, and suffer. Depending upon our wounds and whether or not our self-image is praised or rejected, our moods travel from elation to depression and back again; this can be the source of great emotional instability and pain. The meek person has fought to tame the roaring lion of the human ego, the source of his childish reactions and unreasonable attitudes—the beast that seeks to glorify and defend itself at all costs.

Our greatest human example of meekness is Our Lady. For her, the artifice of ego was never erected. It never claimed anything for itself, for it was dead. If Mary was praised, she gave all glory to God; if she was calumniated, it meant nothing; if she received food, she thanked God; if she went hungry, she blamed no one, least of all her Lord. What could offend a woman who felt like she had no rights? For her, all was gift and grace. Her ego was like fallen timber. If a log receives a devastating blow from an axe, it does not feel anything. It does not react. It is dead. Detached from the world. Attached to God.

The meek person knows how much he is cherished by God; he knows how safe he is in the Lord's love, no matter what happens to the body. The meek one knows that his worth comes solely from God, not from any human opinion—not even his own. *"Blessed are the meek, for they shall inherit the earth"* (Matthew 5:5).

15th Star

FORTITUDE

(one of the four Cardinal Virtues and one of the Seven Gifts of the Holy Spirit)

More than any other phrase in Scripture, Lord, You tell us not to be afraid. If this is so, then why do I suffer from worry and insecurity in my dark interior rooms, where shadows whisper, "You are not safe" and "Brace yourself for stark tomorrows"? How can I, with King David, affirm with defiance:

> The LORD is my light and my salvation;
> whom should I fear?
> The LORD is my life's refuge;
> of whom should I be afraid?
> When evildoers come at me
> to devour my flesh,
> These my enemies and foes
> themselves stumble and fall.
> Though an army encamp against me,
> my heart does not fear;
> Though war be waged against me,
> even then do I trust.
>
> One thing I ask of the LORD; this I seek:
> To dwell in the LORD's house
> all the days of my life,

To gaze on the LORD's beauty,
to visit his temple.
For God will hide me in his shelter
in time of trouble,
He will conceal me in the cover of his tent;
and set me high upon a rock.
Even now my head is held high
above my enemies on every side!
I will offer in his tent
sacrifices with shouts of joy;
I will sing and chant praise to the LORD.
(Psalm 27: 1-6)

My courage depends upon whether or not I live in faith. You, Jesus, must be my brother; You, Father, have to be my Father; you, and You, Holy Spirit, my Spirit. Envelope me, God, pervade me, breathe inside of me, then yes . . . afraid of what? Whom? God is the Omnipotent One, and that Omnipotence lives and breathes within me! Only when I fully embrace and believe this, will I stand against the enemies of my soul and shout with glorious liberty: "Who can be against me?"

16th Star

CONSTANCY

I have sought out distractions and worldly comforts to ease my restlessness, loneliness, sorrow, and ennui. I have spent countless hours before the media and sunk into poor habits, which offend You. My mind tries to pray, but liquid crystal displays on the computer, the television, and the silver screen replay for me their scenes of hollow promises.

But now I see that those hours of escape have not nurtured my soul. In my emptiness, I am turning to You, once again, as my solace, my very Life. While I may never believe or feel that I've "arrived" in prayer or gotten it "just right," I trust that in my striving to come close to You, even amidst my distractions, You smile at my efforts and thank me.

If you, God, are all that matters, if You are the source of my joys, my loved ones, and every goodness that comes to me, why can I not find at least a half hour each day to commune with You in private? Would I not seek this with You, if I could but see You in the flesh? Would I not want You all to myself day and night? Would I not step away from all the false glitter into Your true light? Awaken my spiritual senses to know by faith that You are always there, waiting patiently for me to stop, turn, notice, and encounter.

17th Star

GOODNESS

"*But to you who hear I say, love your enemies, do good to those who hate you, bless those who curse you, pray for those who mistreat you. . . Do to others as you would have them do to you. For if you love those who love you, what credit is that to you? Even sinners love those who love them*" (Luke 6: 27-28, 31-32).

St. Francis de Sales once said, "*You learn to speak by speaking, to study by studying, to run by running, to work by working; and just so, you learn to love by loving. All those who think to learn in any other way deceive themselves*" (The Spirit of Saint Francis de Sales)

So how might you put this kind of goodness into practice?

Let us say a person you had hoped would befriend or date you, a person you trusted, has betrayed your affection. Harness the aggressive waves you wish to send them (which only harm you), and immerse your thoughts towards them in goodness; love them tirelessly.

You receive a negative shock from someone—work to calm yourself and send waves of love to that person. Flee from serious abuse, always; but in your heart, if not in gesture, surround them with affection.

Someone has spoken ill of you? No matter. Retreat into love. Beloved, do not look for revenge but leave room for the wrath; for it is written, "Vengeance is mine, I will repay, says the Lord." Rather, "if your enemy is hungry, feed him; if he is thirsty, give him something to drink; for by so doing you will heap burning coals upon his head." Do not be conquered by evil but conquer evil with good (Romans 12: 19-21). Leave justice to God and treat your enemy as you would the Lord, Jesus. Then there will be no need to even forgive.

"This is unthinkable madness," you say. And so it is. But this is the Lord's therapy, His means of liberating you immediately from the suffering that comes from others. When you have been hurt, do not be alarmed by the storm that may rise within you. Say, "My God, calm the crashing waves, dispel the dark clouds, and erase the lightning flashing through my mind." Then allow time to pass in order to find a place of inner calm. Before the eyes of your soul, see the humble and tender figure of Jesus, silent before the judges, sensitive before the traitor, and say, "Jesus, enter into my being; pour Yourself into my heart; help me to be like You and respond to evil with goodness."

18ᵗʰ Star

SELF-CONTROL

To be human is to possess an area of solitude in our personal makeup. No one but God has access to this solitude, and no one ever will. It is what makes us entirely separate from one another.

No scene can bring this reality to the forefront more than imagining myself on my deathbed. I am surrounded by loved ones, people who know me most intimately, and yet, in spite of all their loving care and heartfelt words, I will, at this moment, be alone, totally alone. Not one person is "with me" in the innermost regions of my being, and no one can accompany me in my death.

Glimpses of such existential aloneness come to me at the hour of an impactful decision, or of assuming an important responsibility. I must ask you, Mary, how did you do it? When the angel Gabriel appeared, an immense wall of historical responsibility rose before you, and you had to decide whether or not to climb it—alone. Your life could proceed quietly if you said no. To say yes meant chaos would shatter your well-ordered and serene life. To bear a child before marriage implied that Joseph would divorce you; you could be stoned to death due to presumed adultery; you would be socially marginalized and stigmatized, labeled with the most offensive name a woman could be given at that time: "harufa"—the raped one. Mary, how is it that under such tremendous pressure you did not dissolve emotionally? Why did your nerves not give way? How did you maintain such self-control? Why did you not try to run and hide and forget?

51

The burden of responsibility always brings with it the burden of solitude, and you had to carry this burden completely alone because it regarded something that would happen once and only once, for the first time and never again. If the news became known, no one would ever believe you. They would say that you had lost your mind.

I am overwhelmed and awed by your maturity. You were but around fourteen! Conscious of the gravity of the encounter with the angel and of your decision, you stood there alone, without consulting anyone, without a single manifestation of human support, and you took the risk of saying the "yes" of your life without any other motive than your faith and your love. All of history could never gather enough praise to appreciate and admire such grandeur.

19ᵗʰ Star

ATTENTIVENESS

To be attentive to Jesus means to accept others. When I am not present to the Lord, I can build walls of separation between myself and those around me—heavy bricks stacked high, made up of fear, animosity, misunderstanding, discord, and aversion.

When I am attentive to Jesus, I am better able to show interest in the human family. Each person is a delicate and precious gem deserving of my undivided attention when I am with them. By virtue of being created in the image of God, they merit the same attention that I desire for myself. If I were speaking to a famous person whom I admired, I would naturally be fully present and alive to that moment. But it is not only in that sports figure or brilliant musician that the Lord has found a home. God's indwelling presence graces every soul. Even the people I cannot bear possess His love. It may be hidden, it may be scarred, it may be twisted, but it is there.

To pay attention to Jesus requires that I ignore when someone stops talking to me, and I continue to speak nicely to him and of him. . . I remain silent amidst a storm of gossip, or speak favorably of the accused. . . I leave the company of those I enjoy to converse with someone I dislike.

When I am present to others the way that You would be, Jesus, they will begin to know You through me, and the fountain of Your love within them will again begin to flow. This requires that I change the way I marginalize, categorize, and socialize with the human family. At the end of the day, help me, Lord, to think not of that person whom I treated the best, but of that person whom I treated the worst, because how I treated that person is how I treated You (Matthew 25:40).

In other words, I am attentive to Jesus when I respect and revere my brother or sister, as if he were Christ Himself, and I silence my base and self-centered impulses. I attend to the Lord when I move, speak, and react, asking myself all the while, what He would do, how He would be, in the same situation. By living in such a way, I am shouting to the world, without a sound, that Jesus Christ lives.

20th Star

FAITH

(one of the three Theological Virtues)

In the vicissitudes of life, any one of us may unexpectedly be under fire by a squadron of arguments, illnesses, disruptions, injustices, and/or misfortunes.

We naturally search for causes and consequences, logical explanations mixed with suspicions and conjectures, and we attribute and distribute blame in all directions. As a result of our analyses, there arises a violent reaction within our hearts; impulses of fury, discouragement, and revenge are quickly released. . . And thus continues the ancient story of the vast majority of humanity.

Against this way of analyzing and responding, which sinks mankind into the kingdom of animals, there is a view that telescopes below the surface of things and sees reality through the lens of faith. Our only enduring consolation is this vision wherein we peacefully accept life's inevitabilities, seeing behind all appearances the Hand which designs and coordinates, permits and oversees everything that happens in the world. If we but catch a glimpse of the power and tenderness of the Father, Who allows this or that misfortune because it will bring about a greater good, then tensions calm, nerves relax, and rebellion transforms into peace.

No unexpected event or painful emergency in the world can shatter the emotional and spiritual stability of those who live in the light of great faith. They are invincible.

55

21st Star

COUNSEL

(one of the seven gifts of the Holy Spirit)

"*When they hand you over, do not worry about how to you are to speak or what you are to say. For it will not be you who speak but the Spirit of Your Father speaking through you.*" (Matthew 10:19). The world needs people with the gift of counsel, witnesses to the commandments, to all that Christ taught us. With the gift of counsel, a person can judge rightly and promptly. The Holy Spirit instantly enlightens the heart regarding what he is to say or do, and through His gift, the Spirit wishes to advise others—even when the message may be wildly unpopular.

The problem is, we, as Catholics, often lack character. We see all about us things that appall and distress our souls, yet we remain mute. Has God not given us tongues and the gift of speech? Then we must speak. Has God not given us multiple and creative means of communicating His Truth with love? Then we must share it. And if the Holy Spirit does not prompt us with strong words against a wrongdoing in a particular moment, then He asks us to address Him quietly within our hearts, calling down merciful rain from heaven upon the offenders. By this, we will win merits for ourselves and nourish the soil of their soul.

Quite simply, we need to form solid, Christ-like characters. Our mere presence should be a form of counsel. It should be enough to signal that certain types of behavior and conversations are good and others are not acceptable. To say it another way: A mother is in a room with her baby, who is just beginning to crawl. The little child sees a fire in the corner of the room and delights in the sparks. She says to herself, "I must go over and play with that!" The little child crawls toward the heat and the light, and the mother suddenly sees where she is headed. She knows that if she doesn't reach her before the girl reaches the fire, her daughter will get burned, and the mother acts, even though the child will likely misunderstand the mother's goodwill and intent.

A mother looks out for all her children in this way. She makes herself aware of the appealing, bright traps that the evil one is setting for them. What the children are seeing may appear attractive, but if they dive into its flames, they are going to get hurt.

22nd Star

RENUNCIATION

Lord, help me to be stern with myself. When self-love and sin stir up temptation, help me to say no. When my body yearns for that which harms it, and my desires override Your commandments, help me to preserve my soul. Save me from myself when gluttony threatens to replace Your indwelling Spirit, and addiction threatens to reduce my soul to a barren, moaning, grasping, desert.

Help me to say no when negativity and anxieties pursue me like a pack of hounds—when envy eats away at my joy, and gossip burns my tongue.

You have told me that I cannot serve both God and mammon, and yet I forge ahead, ignoring Your Word, believing I can do both. I am ensnared by mammon's trap of false promises and artificial support. I am either too frugal or too extravagant, too worried about money or too relaxed. Help me to renounce the god of money, and let my every purchase, my every payment, every drop of my income, follow Your will.

When others speak unfavorably of me, preserve my heart from pride, sadness, indignation, or revenge. Close my mouth, calm my heart, and hold me tight as I allow my disordered self-love to bleed to death. Light a lamp, oh God, under my dark intentions, and expose the lies I hide, even from myself. Illuminate my mind with the stars of self-reflection.

Tear down my ego, which now asks for empathy and later will demand a moment of satisfaction. Help me to go deaf when it cries out for a defense and begs me not to leave it ridiculed. It fools me in the name of reason and objectivity and tells me not to confuse humility with humiliation. Help me to renounce this endless stream of explanations, excuses, and justifications that shout at me! Quiet them once and for all and encourage me to humbly and peacefully accept the truth. My ego calls out a hundred reasons why I had to sin. But my spirit will never be able to give You one excuse.

23rd Star

SURRENDER

A moment of surrender to God's will contains the purest expression of sacrificial, gospel love. Within every act of surrender is a dying to all that is destructive within, be it shame, rage, fear, resentment, sadness, repugnance. . . To say, *"Not as I will, but as you will"* (Matthew 26:39b, Luke 22:42b, Mark 14:36b), starves the heart's aggressive and regressive impulses.

"Sufficient for a day is its own evil" (Matthew 6:34b), and every day forces a Christian to abide in an attitude of surrender, or to live in constant stress because at any moment, annoyances, misunderstandings, setbacks, sicknesses, disappointments, and deceptions may suddenly arise. The believer, after working to resolve whatever can be done, falls into and relies on the strong and all-loving arms of the Father, Who arranges and permits everything.

In the experience of surrender, failures cease to be failures, and death is no longer death. In the total abandonment to God, serenity is born, complexes disappear, and bitterness turns into sweetness. The surrendered person lays her head on the bosom of the Father, accepting His will, and she remains in peace, able to live freely and happily. She sees the fires of anguish turn to dust and ashes, and her fears of the future fly away with the wind. There is no more effective analgesic for the pains and discontent of life than *"Thy will be done"* (Matthew 6:10a).

24th Star

FRIENDLINESS

It is so easy to be friendly. Actions and attitudes that express affection—a smile, a gesture, a look, a pat on the back, a question: "How are you?"—change the course of history. To make someone happy can take but a second! How life-giving, even stupendous, it can be to approach a person in distress and say, "Don't be afraid, my friend; all this will pass. Count on me!" While no blueprint exists for friendliness, what is important, based on the way we treat others, is that the person perceives that I am with him, or I value him.

We can spend a good deal of our time and attention looking to others to see who might fulfill us, searching for a friendly word or a break from the monotony of the day, checking voicemails, e-mails, texts. . . How selfless and gracious is the person who spends as much or more time in such activities doling out messages of consolation, hope, and goodwill. All it takes is a turning away from self to the other.

Simply being happy, even without the intention of spreading cheer, breeds joy. In a study that followed the happiness of nearly 5,000 individuals over twenty years, researchers discovered that when an individual becomes cheerful, the network effect can be measured up to three degrees.[1] Like the extending ripples from a stone tossed in a pond,

---

[1] "Dynamic spread of happiness in a large social network: longitudinal analysis over 20 years in the Framingham Heart Study," by researchers Nicholas Christakis, a Harvard Medical School professor, and James Fowler, a political scientist from the

one person's happiness triggers a chain reaction that benefits not only his friends, but their friends' friends, and so on— the trickling effects lasting for up to one year.

When we become joyful, our next-door neighbors have a 34 percent higher chance of becoming happy themselves, a spouse experiences an 8 percent increased chance of greater joy, and for a friend living close by, it is 25 percent. The possibilities go on. . . A friend of that friend has a nearly 10 percent chance of increased happiness, and a friend of that friend has a 5.6 percent increased chance of it.

Within the benevolent dictates of divine providence, joy has greater power than sadness. Interestingly, unhappiness does not spread through social networks as robustly as happiness. Joy, it seems, loves company more than misery, even reaching out to strangers who are two or three degrees removed, and the effect is hardly fleeting.[2]

What a sublime task it is to wrap others in a mantle of joy. What a beautiful profession it is to hand out small portions of hope. Even if we may not be basking in happiness ourselves, it is so easy to lift up others through a friendly compliment: "Everyone loves what you've done . . . I've heard great things about you . . . What a wonderful talent you have. . . You are a blessing . . ."

Friendliness is a sensitive current, warm and deep, that travels the world.

University of California at San Diego. BMJ, December 5, 2008, http://www.bmj.com/content/337/bmj.a2338, accessed June 29, 2016.
[2] Ibid.

25th Star

DILIGENCE

Lord, help me to walk along Your shores of prayer, between the waves of distraction and sands of dryness. Grace me with enduring patience and strength that I may resolutely advance along Your rich landscape of virtues.

Help me to arrange my private prayer life in a disciplined manner, and to diligently cultivate it—never to leave my spiritual practice for a worldly one. Help me to take time each day to be still, to calm the noisy confusion within me, to control my enormous mental energy and simply adore You. Save me from living in the periphery of my soul, which as St. John of the Cross said, is akin to being in a loud, boisterous neighborhood or a busy marketplace. Silence my exterior senses, my fantasies and worries that perturb my perception of inner realities. Quiet my soul, the frontier between God and man, where I can encounter You.

26th Star

RESPECT

The human being is a mystery, a whole universe unto himself. Each and every person is a unique island, never to be repeated throughout all of time. The first step in respecting others is to recognize that I know almost nothing about them because they are hallowed, unknown worlds.

Lack of respect in the private arena of words is called gossip, and we who initiate or take part in it intrude upon the sacred world of others. We step into another's inner sanctuary and hold court, act as judge, condemn, and make public their sentence. Reputations are ruined in a sentence. Peaceful air is now poisoned. They spoke badly of you, so you speak badly of them. Thoughts become bullets that ricochet and kill, and rumors run from mouth to mouth, becoming more exaggerated and distorted each time, like cancerous tumors.

In this state of affairs, no one truly listens to anyone, and no one speaks sincerely. Insecurity and suspicion fog the air and transparency becomes impossible. Bodies sit in open rooms with imaginary doors slammed shut. As a consequence, each soul takes refuge in his or her inner world and outwardly assumes a defensive posture. Like a slow-burning firework, lack of respect sets off sparks of loneliness, evasion, fear, and for its finale, a dazzling display of animosity.

But from the moment we comply with the virtue of mutual respect, and we honor the living mystery of the people God has placed beside us. . . from the moment we choose to bite our anxious tongues and treat others as we would the walking and breathing Jesus. . . seeds of trust are planted, the tree of camaraderie grows, and acceptance and joy flourish in its branches.

27th Star

HOPE

(one of the three Theological Virtues)

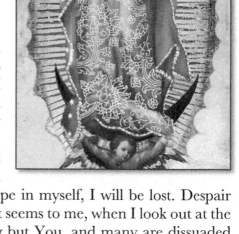

Bring me, Lord, along the path of hope. You are the only One Who can see the way. For all I know, I am taking a detour from a cleared and safe path into blackberry brambles and poison ivy.

I do not know the way and it scares me at times, but I must walk forward in hope. If I place that hope in myself, I will be lost. Despair and pessimism will be my reward. It seems to me, when I look out at the world, that many hope in anything but You, and many are dissuaded from the Way.

Even I make my own goals, draw up my own plans, and lay down the stones of an edifice that seems to have no other architect but me. Save me, save us all, Lord Jesus, from our folly when we put our hope in something other than You: in our ourselves, our reputation, money or power, political leaders or parties, or even in the Hollywood glamour of the world's "stars."

Give me, oh God, the most profound conviction and awareness that I will destroy my future, that the world will destroy itself, if hope in You is not present. Teach me and promise me that in spite of troubled times, weary afternoons, and stark nights that my future and the fate of the Church and the world are secure in Your all-loving, all-powerful hands.

Though I wander through a jungle of camouflaged lies, let me live to see the glow of the Resurrection rising up at the edge of a clear horizon. Give me glimpses of the promised day to come, beautiful beyond dreams. Set my sights on the life of the world beyond, so that my life to be lived now is guided by the unfailing star of hope in You.

28th Star

RESILIENCY

We step into our boss's office for our annual raise, and we receive notice that we're fired. We pick up the phone to hear that our loved one has died in a terrible accident. All the money we invested is gone. The person we had counted on most in life betrays us. A family member or friend commits suicide. Our child falls into a life of serious sin and thinks nothing of it. We receive a diagnosis of a terminal and painful cancer. Is anyone free from these dark and terrible shocks that descend upon us like a hawk, pierce us with their talons, and carry us off into God's silence?

Such moments come to us unbidden. We can be standing erect and strong, rejoicing in the blessings of life, when an unforeseen wrecking ball crashes into our being, shattering our thoughts and senses, and sometimes, the foundation of our existence. We can scarcely move forward, gather up hope or interest in life, when we are experiencing ourselves as a thousand scattered pieces.

The Gospel of Luke tells us that Mary, the Mother of God, despite her exalted status, was not immune to such crushing blows. Ponder how she must have felt when she lost her Child for three days in Jerusalem—a prefiguring of the time she would lose Him for three days to the clutches of death. Her Son was no one less than the Savior of the world, and the Creator had entrusted her and Joseph to care for and protect Him. Imagine her panic when Jesus, a budding teenager, could not be found in the men's caravan, nor was He seen in the women's. Setting out on the first caravan back to Jerusalem, Mary began her anxious search of three days and three nights.

She must have retraced her steps innumerable times, scouring the courtyards and streets, running in the wrong direction, turning her head to look left, when perhaps she should have looked right. No doubt she made a thousand inquiries, all with the same answer: "No, I haven't seen him." Had He fallen into the hands of His enemies? Was He alive? Would she ever see Him again? Why was God so silent? Why wouldn't He just tell her through an angel what had happened to her Son?

After three days of little eating and less sleep, Mary finally found her beloved Child. Do you believe her first reaction was joy? It was not. Her words were a reprimand, a release of painful emotion: "Son, why have you done this to us? Your father and I have been looking for you with great anxiety."

The youthful Jesus answered her in a seemingly unconcerned, nonchalant fashion, almost as if He were putting the blame back onto her. *"Why were you looking for me? Did you not know that I must be in my Father's house?"* (Luke 2:49)

Then Scripture says another remarkable thing. In a weave of different translations, the Gospel says: *His mother stored/kept/treasured/pondered these things in her heart* (Luke 2:51b). The moments that followed the end of Mary's nightmare give us a glimpse into her resilience. After three days and nights without much food, sleep, or rest, with her mind tortured by fear and uncertainty, her body exhausted—and in spite of receiving such a disconcerting response, she retired in peaceful surrender and repose in order to treasure her Son's words in her heart.

Such resiliency could only come from a heart that is dead to self-satisfaction. Only those who have died to the demands of ego can go peacefully to where the aftermath of shock takes them and immediately absorb the healing power of God. Mary did not put up a barrier to grace by becoming indignant or full of accusations or self-blame, nor did she become fearful of the future. Instead, she allowed herself to relax and be restored in the will of the Father. Tomorrow was a new day . . . one that could again be filled with peace.

29th Star

DETACHMENT

We live our first years of human life learning how to attach to people and things. The happiest and most well-adjusted children first attach themselves to at least one loving caregiver, as if that person were their own body. To eat, the baby latches onto the mother's breast or a bottle. To find comfort, the child cries until she is picked up and cuddled. Through trust and dependence, this attachment ideally continues.

From a very young age, we discover that certain things, both within and outside of ourselves, please us and give us a happy sensation; and other things strike us as unpleasant. To navigate the physical world as toddlers, we reach for and grab objects, becoming attached to our favorite ones, hence the beloved "blankie." We put unsavory objects in our mouths and spit them out with distaste. Naturally, we grow to savor the things we enjoy, even some of our own personal traits, and we become possessively attached to them. When those things that are pleasurable to us are threatened or in danger of going away, we become distraught. Suddenly fear, which discharges aggressive energy in defense of the threatened possession, seizes us, and war is born.

The only way to win this war is through holy detachment. Unwelcome lessons in detachment have followed us from the moment we were painfully expelled from the womb—our warm and familiar first home. We entered this world crying. As babies, we felt that our caregivers were physical extensions of ourselves, so it caused us tremendous inner conflict when they did not come on demand, comfort us properly in our wounds, or supply the "right" kind of food at the "right" time. Through disappointment and struggle, we learned that what we thought was part of ourselves was a separate entity with its own mind. Thus began a lifetime of lessons in the virtue of detachment, culminating in the release of the last attachment of all, the attachment to our very life.

St. John of the Cross tells us that freedom from all attachments, even the smallest, is necessary to attain divine union, the highest goal of every human soul. Attachments, he says, can range from serious sin to seemingly harmless preferences:

Some examples of these habitual imperfections are: the common habit of being very talkative; a small attachment one never really desires to conquer, for example, to a person, to clothing, to a book or a cell, or to the way food is prepared, and to other trifling conversations and little satisfactions in tasting, knowing, and hearing things, and so on. . . As long as this attachment remains, it is impossible to make progress in perfection, even though the imperfection may be very small.

It makes little difference whether a bird is tied by a thin thread or by a cord. Even if it is tied by thread, the bird will be held bound just as surely as if it were tied by cord; that is, it will be impeded from flying as long as it does not break the thread. Admittedly the thread is easier to break, but no matter how easily this may be done, the bird will not fly away without first doing so. This is the lot of those who are attached to something: No matter how much virtue they have, they will not reach the freedom of the divine union. (*The Ascent of Mt. Carmel*)

30th Star

POVERTY

Lord, free me from the seduction and fleeting comfort of materialism, which few people ever confess. Even the rich man who saw Your face and heard Your words, *"Sell all that you have and distribute it to the poor, and you will have a treasure in heaven. Then come, follow me"* (Luke 18:22b), grew sad and walked away. Protect me from fearful thoughts that hiss in my ears, "God will not provide," for they keep me from giving away what I do not need. Free me from the whispers caressing me with delusion: "It is God who has blessed you with many possessions. You have worked hard and deserve to keep and enjoy what you've earned." Is the poor woman stooped over in the heat of the fields day after day, her hands afflicted with sores and arthritis from fruit-picking, any less deserving? Has she not spent herself in long years of hard labor, as well?

Who are the poor, Lord? You were among them, and You were a brother to them. Your mother, too, was poor. From the heights of your divinity, where You reigned over all, You descended to the dregs of earth, where You had nowhere to lay your head. You, the King of all richness, stripped yourself of heaven, imprisoned yourself in the human body, and having come of age, left everything, even Your poor home and beloved Mother, to preach the Good News. Being the center of all that is, You made Yourself most present with those on the outskirts, the throwaways, the cast aside. You paid special care to those who were hungry, needy, ill, too young, too elderly, forgotten—and You still do.

Who are the poor, Lord? You say I must help them. I see Your poor in the faces of those who have little to nothing in this world. I see them on the streets, searching through garbage, working thankless jobs for little pay. But I know that they are everywhere: in those who are ignored because they have no noticeable beauty, talent, or character; in the lonely girl who has lost all sense of self-worth; in the narcissistic man who thinks to speak only of himself; in the woman surrounded by cigarette butts, who cannot peel herself away from her TV screen.

There are so many poor, Lord; they are legion. Like a swelling tempest, their cry grows more chaotic and insistent each day, with needs bigger than my small heart. Free me from my fear and passivity, Lord, from the excuses that they deserve their lot, that I can do nothing to help them, or am too busy. Oh God, what if that poor person were me?

31st Star

WISDOM

(The first and highest of the seven gifts of the Holy Spirit)

To climb the mountain called faith toward the peak of sanctity, God first leaves the initiative to the soul. In the beginning stages, the soul, aided by His grace, must search for its own means of spiritual wisdom and support. Like a child beginning to walk, the soul looks for and needs such things as psychological crutches, methods of concentration, spiritual exercises, readings, and points for reflection in order to ease forward. God, in return, encourages and helps the soul through personal consolations, and prayer seems more a product of human striving than divine promptings.

As the soul advances through the higher spiritual stages of growth and wisdom, God slowly begins to take up the initiative in the soul and offers special supports and unexpected touches. At these levels, the soul finds the psychological, intellectual, and spiritual aids it used to lean on to be useless crutches. God removes all initiatives away from the soul and subjects it to submission and surrender under the power and guidance of the Holy Spirit. Once the Spirit bursts into the scene, the soul feels the need to purify itself through mortifications and detachment. Eventually, the dark night falls, leaving the soul without consolation, but at the very doorstep of union with God. When the trial has passed, to the attainment of purity of heart, peace in suffering, freedom from the world, and infused with divine wisdom, the soul finds itself able to advance without any obstacle towards the transforming union.

While the person who prays scales the cliffs of divine heights, formerly unknown powers may emerge within the soul. Fueled by grace, these powers can push the soul up a steep incline into a whirlwind, where God becomes more and more the All and the Absolute. The whole person is pulled in, taken up, and slowly transformed into a torch, which warms, burns, and illuminates. Its final end is to know God Himself.

32nd Star

DISCIPLINE

Rules of training are equally valid for athletics as they are for the spirit. "Swim fifty laps!" someone calls out to you. "Not happening!" you shout back. But you begin, slowly at first, doing very little and finding yourself quickly out of breath. You continue over time, advancing week after week, adding more speed, developing greater endurance and capacity. Then one day, it happens. You wake up and have little to no difficulty doing what once seemed impossible.

All of us carry within us, within our genetic code and our soul's core, unique spiritual capacities and divine talents, which may today be asleep, or perhaps atrophied, but tomorrow may bloom. When we exercise our innate gifts in prayer and action, our attraction and desire for God awakens, and the Lord becomes more and more our satisfaction and our all. Everything comes alive. Sacraments are no longer stale rituals and empty sayings, but spiritual banquets. Chastity is no longer unhealthy repression but mysterious fulfillment. Daily duties, be they of God, are no longer meaningless drudgery but a mission. . . the beatitudes no longer absurd paradoxes but deep wells of wisdom and fulfillment.

When I do not train my spirit to swim with God, He is, at best, an empty word, a "Mr. Nobody"—at worst, a dark and foreboding sea. But when I plunge into His living waters, God becomes "Someone." The deeper I dive and the further I swim, the more the mystery of His love envelops and enraptures me.

I begin in a dark room. I see nothing. I decide to strike a match. In prayerful supplication, I kneel at my bedside. Tired and distraught, I push myself to attend morning Mass. Tempted by fleeting pleasures of the world, I beg Jesus to live and breathe in me. My small light brightens. Suddenly, a colorful picture is revealed on the wall. Light flickers and dances across the corner of a table. A chandelier sparkles above me. In time, I find more and more ways to bring greater light into the room. One day, I look around and gasp, "Oh, the room is beautiful, so beautiful!"

Did the room change? No. It was the same as it had always been and always will be. But as I stepped into the light of God's presence, new perspectives and shapes and sights, all previously unknown to me, began to appear.

Not all saints, prophets, and martyrs were exceptional beings because they were born into the world that way. Many of them had to maintain a relentless struggle in their process of sanctification. Through their efforts, the law of attraction between masses was fulfilled: the greater their proximity to the Light of God, the greater the velocity between the two. The closer we get to union with the divine, so grows God's attraction, His seduction, and our desire.

The beautiful room never changed. It never will. But I can.

33rd Star

MORTIFICATION

Lord Jesus, fashion me into Your likeness. Mold me into a being who, like St. Paul said, fills up in his flesh what is lacking in the afflictions of Christ on behalf of His body, which is the Church (Colossians 1:24a). Though your Sacrifice lacks nothing in its total gift, the Church body must undergo redemptive suffering to fulfill Your work on Earth.

So inspire me to lavish You with gifts, intentional acts of self-denial and courage, all wrapped in small sufferings. Help me to harness my anger and hold my tongue when I am tempted to chastise, to praise You when I feel crushed by the weight of the cross, and to hand You my hurt from unjust words and unfavorable opinions. Give me the strength to deny myself a savory morsel of food or refreshing drink, to reach out to those who are materially or spiritually poor, and to finally act on what I have avoided, but know I must do.

Motivate me, Lord, to intercede for those who feel no need for prayer, to love those whose hearts have frozen, and to have hope for those whose aspirations have been dashed on jagged rocks.

Through my gifts of self-mortification, may I harness the unruly and unforeseen currents of destruction that are sweeping through the world and the Church. May I help You replant Your peaceful garden. The beautiful rose bushes with the most piercing thorns are supplied well-enough by You, Lord, but I will never cease to concern myself with the little flowers, those that collect the dew and reflect the glory of the sun.

34th Star

BOLDNESS

To live in the consuming fire of the Holy Trinity is to feel no peace unless one shares the Good News. Like St. Paul, the cry of a heart in love is, *"Woe to me if I do not preach the gospel"* (1 Corinthians 9:16b). Refashioned by the hand of the Divine Potter into the likeness of God, the soul cannot help but long for the whole world to be saved and to ardently wish that at the name of Jesus, every knee should bend and tongue confess that Jesus Christ is Lord (Philippians 2:10-11).

If the fire to evangelize is not present within, something carnal and worldly has overshadowed the expansive light of the indwelling Spirit, Who is forever active and creative in spreading the Kingdom. If we are fully alive and docile to His promptings—at times felt as inspiration, at others as nagging discomfort—we will share through word, deed, and prayer the numerous treasures of God and His Church. Temptations of fear . . . complacency . . . judgment . . . anger . . . pride . . .cannot prevent us from moving outside of our personal comfort and taking the necessary risks to save souls.

The world is filled with people who are lost and wandering, chasing shadows that lead to the total loss of light. Not many know the why of their existence. Without authentic witness and bold evangelization, there is no future for them, and there is no future for the Catholic Church.

Make careful note of this: effective witness can only come from an intimate and vital relationship with Jesus. Just as He affirmed, "I came from the Father and have come into the world" (John 16:28a), so too, in order to have the moral authority, authentic credibility, and divine power to act as witnesses, we must be able to repeat: "I have been with the Father, and I come to tell you what I have seen and heard."

35th Star

UNDERSTANDING

(one of the seven gifts of The Holy Spirit)

God is normally logical within Himself. This aspect of the Creator can be terribly difficult to accept, and our faith can be violently shaken when events follow to their natural conclusions.

"How horrible! That drunk driver ran over a small boy and killed him. His mother had no one else in her life but him!" Was God vicious, vindictive, perhaps evil? What happened? The simplistic answer: God allowed the universal law of action and consequence, physics and velocity, impaired reflexes from alcohol consumption, to continue to function, and as a result, tragedy occurred. Like Martha at the tomb of Lazarus, we cry out in protest, *"Lord, if you had been here, my brother would not have died"* (John 11:21).

So we question God: "Lord, could You not have prevented such a calamity?" Speaking in absolute terms, the answer is yes, because the Creator of all laws and of time itself can rescind and warp them at will. But He rarely does this. He respects His creation and the laws that He set in motion.

I may not fully understand why He allowed the nightmare or how He plans to bring a greater good out of it, but I understand that He will do so. I understand that He will do so because He is all good. I also understand that He allowed the untimely, unjust, horrific, and preventable, cold-blooded torture and murder of His only Son at the hands of those He created and loved "to death"—only because a greater good would come from it. God will never allow a negative unless it will lead to a greater positive. This is a law that God has set in motion, and one that He will never rescind. The gift of understanding also assures me that the greatest good of all is not the salvation of temporal bodies, but of eternal souls.

Therefore, I will silence my worry, adopt a spiritual perspective, and cease to ask why, because I understand, I truly understand, that all will be well. All will be well.

Receive the sacrament of reconciliation this week in preparation for consecration

36th Star

PRUDENCE

(one of the four Cardinal Virtues)

Prudence sees the world from a lofty vantage point. Standing like a towering redwood, stately and statuesque, it governs over the smaller virtues, the pines and oaks, dictating how they are to be used. It judges rightly between good and evil and discerns what is great above what is good.

Of its many dictates, prudence tells when to move into decisive action and when to lie down in surrender. At critical moments, we can come face to face with extremely bothersome, unjust, or harmful life circumstances. Prudence compels us to ask, "Can this thing which hurts me be changed or bettered? Does it have a solution? And if so, is the solution something I should attempt?"

Prudence guides our best assessment, in keeping with Church teachings and Holy Scripture, aided by research, prayer, and wise counsel. If a worthwhile solution—however small—appears on the horizon, prudence will join with fortitude and say, "It is not time to surrender for any reason. It is time to fight with all of your weapons at hand and to excite your energies into play."

When looking at reality, however, we too often discover that a great many of life's thorns have no remedy or recourse, or if there is a solution, it does not lie within our grasp. These are the "impossibilities" of life. If there is nothing that we can do in a situation, then it is futile to cry over it. To resist with all one's soul a fait accompli is a suicidal act, causing a violent mental reaction. It leaves us indignant, afraid, sad, blaming, embittered; and the more we resist, the more the situation oppresses us. Before long, we are trapped in a self-destructive cycle, which spins us into depressive or anxious states. We can live obsessed with that which we cannot alter, and precisely because we reject it, it becomes a fixed attachment in our minds.

In the end, when faced with life's dead ends, we have only two choices: to surrender or explode. Those who are prudent say to themselves, "It is useless to weep and complain. From this moment on, I will bend the knees of my spirit and lay my head on Your breast, Lord. I surrender this problem to You. It is Yours to take care of, not mine."

At this, God raises up the prudent far above the vicissitudes of life into a gentle stream of peace, where nothing can trap them, not disappointment or success, adversity or prosperity, discomfort or ease.

37th Star

PIETY

(one of the seven gifts
of The Holy Spirit)

The pious may travel the same road as the impious, but they see the surrounding landscape entirely differently. They walk into gardens and notice that the flowers speak, the birds sing, even the insects chirp, telling of God's love. The impious notice the flowers, but focuses on the mud on their shoes, the gardener's mistakes, and the hot sun burning their necks, all of which close their hearts to God and remind them that beauty comes tainted with annoyance and pain.

The pious ponder the Good News preached by the One who came from the Father's House, Who said that the Kingdom is like a jewel that projects a light different from the sun's, a light infinitely more resplendent than a sunrise—a splendor so rich that to possess it is worth selling everything. The impious do not wish to sell for they see only loss and no reward.

The pious honor the holy and run to fulfill their sacred duties. The impious find religious obligation an impediment to freedom and a lackluster chore. While the pious give to God what is God's and to Caesar what is Caesar's, the impious give to Caesar what is God's alone.

The pious and the impious descend together into the same deep valleys of injustice and woe: gorgeous mansions touching miserable shacks; racist collisions and sexual abuse; state-sponsored death from the newly conceived to the elderly; the marriage of what is spiritually forbidden; the flaunting of hedonism before children's eyes. Both the pious and impious may believe that the trajectory of the world is a downward curve.

But piety is not naiveté, and impiety sees wrongly. As the pious walk along the valley floor, they see evil but know the dawn will appear and be triumphant. Their penetrating glance of faith captures luminous rays hidden from the human retina. The impious see evil and know that goodness does not always win. They contemplate how by late afternoon the sky will darken, and soon the night's firmament will be void of stars.

For both, the day of death will arrive. In contemplation of the resplendent Face of God, the pious will see that their most extravagant dreams were insignificant alongside the glory of a Presence that satiates all desire. The impious will see that their vision was a smokescreen, which hardly resembled reality at all.

38th Star

JUSTICE

"*He came to Nazareth, where he had grown up, and went according to his custom into the synagogue on the sabbath day. He stood up to read and was handed a scroll of the prophet Isaiah. He unrolled the scroll and found the passage where it was written:*

"The Spirit of the Lord is upon me,
because he has anointed me
to bring glad tidings to the poor.
He has sent me to proclaim liberty to captives
and recovery of sight to the blind,
to let the oppressed go free,
and to proclaim a year acceptable to the Lord."
(Luke 4:16-20)

When Jesus rolled up the scroll, handed it back to the attendant, and sat down, the eyes of all in the synagogue looked intently at Him. In that pivotal moment of human history, who was Jesus concerned for?

When a man is wrongfully imprisoned because of the color of his skin, that person touches, breathes, and imbibes injustice. When a woman works long hours away from her unsupervised children but still cannot feed them, she lives without reprieve in the worry and despair of injustice. When a young girl is sold into sexual slavery, she is strapped to a pillar and whipped by injustice. They have no voice.

Jesus unrolled the scroll and said, "*Today this scripture passage is fulfilled in your hearing*" (Luke 4:21). In other words, "Today, and from this moment forward, I am your voice"—a voice that echoes through time in the mouths of the Lord's disciples. These are the disciples who speak words of golden hope for the mute and unheard: the imitators of the One who stands in defense of the homeless, the poor, the unborn, the elderly, the children, the sick, the mentally ill, the abused. These are the tall trees with sacred roots in whose canopy of welcoming branches, delicate birds take up their nests.

These men and women know that in whatever state of life they find themselves, they are God's children before all else. They are not doctors who are Catholic, but Catholics who are doctors. They are not mothers who are Catholic, but Catholic mothers. Their "yes" is a song in God's ear when the world falls silent, and their "no" is a spear in God's hand when the world sleeps with its enemy. To every task they bring a supernatural outlook and to every person God's love. They follow where Christ leads them, even if it may cost them their very lives. All of this they do because love and justice demand it. They have unrolled and read the scroll, and God's voice is theirs.

39th Star

PEACE

The longing for peace stirs in the soul of every human being. It is a persistent call to an inner existence far different from the restless dissatisfaction that runs through the countless souls roaming this Earth. Those few who have found a sanctuary of serenity within have conquered the self in a hidden, personal battle of mythic proportions. Crucified to themselves, having turned their wills entirely over to God, they live in the dwelling of peace.

The strings of their hearts pulse in unison with the Creator in harmonious melodies heard only by them; the world's trifles and trends disappear for them and are no longer of interest. Their manner is thoughtful and courteous. They are sensitive in nature; the problems of others become theirs. With thoughts positive and pure, even toward their enemies, they dedicate their time to pray for them, rather than criticize and condemn.

The enemy lies in the depths of human hearts, not on the lands of opposing nations. People of peace cannot be people of war, for the will of God has no aggression or brutality contained within it. Hidden in the thoughts of man are wars that distort the values of God with compromise to the point that leaders and peoples and nations burst forth with violence, ruining human destinies and choking the planet. *You shall not kill* (Exodus 20:30) is not a commandment overturned suddenly by a declaration of war.

Our Lady, when she appeared in Fatima, gave us a somber warning: "War is a punishment for sin." The Lord of All and His gracious Mother are not relying on our weapons to bring us peace and salvation. They are relying on our prayers, our Rosaries, our fasting and sacrifices, and our holy lives. Jesus is the Prince of Peace, not the prince of war. Mary is the Queen of Peace, not the queen of war.

Day and night, let us commit to delving deeper within ourselves in order to douse the persistent flames of pride and cut off the thousand heads of anger, aggression, and revenge. For the enemy is not just without. He is within. Only when we have conquered ourselves and silenced our fears will the world rest in the hands of the God of peace.

40th Star
EXCELLENCE

Many seem intent on living a life filled with ease and pleasures of all kinds. Life, however, was never designed by God to be easy. Even from the first, God made man and woman to work, and work we must.

Many spend their intellectual energies and physical strength hammering against God's Kingdom, whether with clear intention or in the shadows of ignorance. From the rising of the sun and long past its setting hour, they pursue their selfish or misguided ambitions, unearthing the far-reaching dungeons of the netherworld and piling heavy burdens on the shoulders of the holy ones. Using the talents and gifts bestowed upon them by their Creator, they work diligently and intelligently, sometimes unknowingly, to thwart God's plans by fulfilling their own.

To stem this rising tide, God is calling the Catholic world to spread itself like a vast and interlinked system of roots, drawing its nourishment from His living waters. Across sodalities, professions, politics, corporations, networks, and clubs, wherever the Spirit of God plants His people, we must push ourselves up through the earth to grow strong and tall, always reaching for the Son. Only if we grow where we are planted can we change the world.

With the precept in mind that God and family and people remain always our highest priority, God is seeking excellence in our work. If by nature, inheritance, or misfortune, we have difficulties with learning or challenges with expression, God views our struggle and strivings as nothing less than human excellence. If we are able to do well the work He is calling us to, then He expects us to do it well. If we can be one of the best at what we do, then He gives us no excuse for not being so. And those who are the best in their fields or expertise, without Christ in their lives, are only a fraction of what they could be if they possessed the living God. In every holy accomplishment, all glory is God's alone, for we are but dust. His light shines most radiantly through Catholics who know that they are little, giving them the appearance of being great.

Oh, how precious time is! Blessed are those who know how to make good use of it. If all could understand its eternal value, undoubtedly they would do their utmost to spend it in a manner worthy of the saints. Nothing less than the eternal life of souls is at stake. God's pace for our work is steady, never hurried, and at times, we must rest in His love, for the world tires us with its lack of meaningful direction and warped priorities. But rest is not laziness and laxity, which are thieves of the Spirit. God has designed us to plow forever forward, doing one thing at a time and doing it well. If we aim for perfection—not out of a distorted sense of perfectionism, which focuses on the self, but born of a desire to do something beautiful for God—at least we will do our best. And once we have used our talents in His service, with the aid of the human means available to us, all that is left to do is raise our eyes toward heaven and say, "Father, this is my best. I offer it to you. Please accept my lowly gift, and by it, help me and the world to grow evermore in love with You."

41st Star

TEMPERANCE

(one of the four Cardinal Virtues)

Temperance is a curbing of the hunger of the body, the influence of negative emotions, and the self-centered aspirations of the ego. This cardinal virtue, forever gathering other virtues safely beneath its broad wings, protects the soul from the extremes which tempt it. Our flesh, when satiated, finds temporary satisfaction in indulgence, but in time, becomes ever more dissatisfied with the more it attains. Addiction brews, and dark spirits enter our being, gaining control of our faculties and maneuvering us like puppets to achieve their deadly ends.

We can become like hungry wolves, forever seeking to fulfill our perceived needs, and as a result, devour ourselves and others. Material goods and money fool us into thinking they are gods. Food says it will end our emptiness; drugs and alcohol promise us no pain. Power tells us we are less vulnerable and out of control, and painted faces with half-naked bodies parade in our minds as the answer. Entertainment, videogames, the Internet, sports, unhealthy relationships, excessive exercise, and myriads of vanities take up thrones in our souls. Television—the new Blessed Sacrament, which families sit before and adore—infiltrates our minds like an imperceptible, poisonous gas.

The end result: we live with restless bodies, wild emotions, hungry eyes, and salivating mouths, chasing food that doesn't nourish and water that leaves us thirsty. All the while God assures us, if we listen: "You needn't grasp for what I wish to lovingly provide—in My way and My time. Trust Me. Patience and temperance attain all good things."

In temperance, we choose to accept small sufferings in exchange for enduring, horrific, even eternal ones. In this way, we fluster the devil, who is like a mad dog tied by a chain. Beyond the length of his fetters, he cannot catch hold of anyone. But the one who gets too close will be caught. Through the small sufferings demanded by temperance, our souls keep a safe distance.

It is like this. A boy decides not to enter into gossip and thus becomes the gossip of others. Over time, he is praised for his integrity and trustworthiness. A girl declines the sexual advances of boys and suffers their disinterest but saves herself from the ravages of a shattered soul, broken relationships, and perhaps even from abortion. She marries happily. A man refuses to drink heavily with his work buddies and endures the ostracizing of certain friends but spares himself hangovers and the vice grip of addiction and disaster. He leads a fruitful life. A woman abstains from staring at pornography and avoids spending the rest of her days trying to erase the emblazoned images from her mind. She is creative and free.

From temperance springs both pain and joy. In a certain sense, we could maintain that the pain has been conquered, or at least, has lost its most frightening sting—meaninglessness. From the finite suffering that temperance brings, glorious fountains of virtue gush forth, and the higher they reach, the more fertile the subsoil from which they spring. God delights in the temperate soul, offering it answers, flashes of light, and comfort in persecution. A panorama of numerous avenues and transcendent gifts opens up to it because the temperate soul is one God can trust.

42nd Star

CHASTITY

Chastity, for some, is a peaceful state of being, freeing the body from tension and the mind from longing, preparing the soul for ecstatic heights of selfless love. For others, it is a worse fate than the unbridled storms of lust that seek to devour the soul. Chastity and purity too often lie wounded on the side of the road. They are dismissed and discarded in favor of a lonely fire that propels the body to unite with opportunity in its quest for love.

The serpent whispers that to live without sexual pleasure is to live an inhuman, unfulfilled existence in a solitary state of repression and deprivation. A liar from the beginning, the devil fills the soul with suggestive images, words, music, and experiences, in order to trap the senses. The mind and body, thus addicted and possessed, believe and feel that they can no longer live otherwise. Even between husband and wife, where sexual union is meant to mirror the unitive and procreative love of the Trinity, raw sensuality can displace love.

Long forgotten are the innocent joys of youth and the simpler pleasures of life. Never known or seldom remembered is God's clarion call to honor the human body as a living temple of the Holy Spirit. Chastity doesn't dare to use another for pleasure, easement, or an escape from loneliness. It never behaves or dresses so as to seduce or draw salacious attention. Chastity respects oneself and others as dignified creatures made in the image of God. It inspires the squeeze of a hand, the glance of an eye, the embrace of a hug, to heal and never harm. Only can we imagine the tenderness contained in the touches between Joseph and Mary.

"You certainly will not die!" (Genesis 3:4b) "Go ahead and take a bite of the fruit from this tree," urges the serpent, while the purest of them all, the Lady clothed with the sun, warns us not to, as through her appearances in Fatima (1917): *More souls go to hell because of sins of the flesh than for any other reason. . . Certain fashions will be introduced that will offend Our Lord very much. . . Woe to women lacking in modesty. . . The sins of the world are very great. . . If men only knew what eternity is, they would do everything in their power to change their lives.*

Nothing good is lost forever while a soul remains alive. Our spiritual senses can be awakened and the relentless chanting of lust harnessed when we run into the arms of God—to the sacraments, to Scripture, to fasting and prayer—and if needed, to counseling and a program of recovery. In time, the soul will begin to taste the sweet nectar of freedom.

43rd Star

OBEDIENCE

If we are seeking heaven, we have engaged in a dynamic process of transfiguration, or Christification—the exchanging of one figure for another. The more we become like God, the more insatiable is our hunger for virtue, our longing to be a saint. After all, it is for this that we were born, and nothing less than our complete sanctification will ensure our radiant passage through the gates of paradise.

We are creatures who find ourselves alive and here on earth without having opted for this. We did not choose our bodies or the wonderful qualities and dark defects of our personality, encrypted in our DNA before we were born. Nor did we select the natural gifts or oppression inherited from our ancestors. The substitution of one figure for another consists of emptying ourselves of those dark congenital defects in order to replace them, little by little, with the positive aspects of Jesus. It also consists of divesting the clothing of the *"old self"* (Colossians 3:9-10; Ephesians 4:22-24; Romans 6:6), such as pride, selfishness, animosity, or rebelliousness, and then dressing in a new garment not made of this earth.

I must disappear so that Jesus Christ may appear in me. I must vacate my territory so that He may fully occupy it. To this end, Jesus gave us the Catholic Church, which He promised would guide us until the end of time (Matthew 16:18, Daniel 7:13-14). He did not leave us orphans, even though some should seek to destroy the Church from within. He did not give us the Commandments and the Holy Spirit's guidance of the Church in order to deceive us. He did not say, "Some of my teachings are true and some are not—it is up to you, individually, to discern which are which. Best of luck. Your salvation depends on it." Why would an all-loving God deceive us with false moral teachings and thwart our efforts of sanctification? This would make no sense, of course. Jesus promised to never withdraw His hand of moral guidance and authority from the Church, even when certain leaders, themselves, do not follow it.

We are living in an age of disobedience, where some rashly believe that they know better than the Catechism, than Church councils, than the saints, than even Jesus Himself. They twist Scripture to say the opposite of what it has made so clear. They pray that the current winds of change will expose the real truth for the first time, and they believe that the Catholic Church and its holy ones have been living in and teaching apostasy from the beginning. "All were wrong. Scripture is wrong. But I am right."

Those who follow the teachings of the Church, as instituted by Christ, will find harbors of safety and rest for their souls. And those who follow the winds of moral relativism and flow with the current tides of mass disobedience, will be pulled by an undertow into deep and dangerous seas.

44th Star

SACRIFICE

A degenerative disease, a lifeless sacramental marriage, a wayward child, a terrible injustice . . . What is the meaning of such sacrifice and hardship? Of what use is it? When the very first human heart suffered, that was its cry. There is no one who, in a moment of anguish, has not asked the same question, either explicitly, or in a confused way. The darkest tragedy, however, lies not in the suffering in and of itself, but in suffering uselessly.

A girl is abandoned by her father and turns to heroin to ease her pain. She dies from an unplanned overdose, with a needle still protruding from her arm, her cherished dreams dying with her. Such meaningless tribulation in and around us breeds and foments rebellion in the soul to the point that we can become consumed with a futile resentment or a blind rage against life and God.

When Jesus walked this earth, the turbulence and hatred raised in His footsteps were of such magnitude that His life, humanly speaking, went up in flames and turned to ashes, ending in unspeakable calamity and suffering.

The difference? Not a drop of His blood was shed in vain. Every flash of the whip, every blood-curdling scream, every piercing thorn and pernicious insult that stabbed Him was His offering of love for the salvation of the world. And every moment of our suffering is meant to be the same. This is the secret behind all redemptive pain and voluntary sacrifice. *"Come, take up your cross and follow me"* (Mark 8:34), *"When you fast, do not look gloomy like the hypocrites"* (Matthew 6:16a), *". . . calculate the cost*" (Luke 14:28), "*. . .every one of you who does not renounce all his possessions cannot be my disciple*" (Luke 14:28,33). Our suffering can save souls.

Jesus came to heal and alleviate our needless and worthless, self-inflicted pain. He will try, at every turn, to claim our attention and shout, "Wake up! This is needless. You are the cause of your agony!" But when, in communion with the suffering Christ, we offer to God our unavoidable sufferings, meaning is restored and rebellion melts away. As we discover the salvific nature of personal sacrifice carved into the mystery of the cross, we are visited by a mysterious sense of peace and joy.

The time is coming, and it has already come, when believers, in the footsteps of the Master, will no longer be preoccupied with their personal pain, but will stretch out their arms to embrace a suffering humanity and make its wounds their own.

45th Star

MERCY

In the last weeks and days of His life, Jesus was met with indifference, rage, cowardice, and betrayal. Storms gathered around Him and drew near, whispering torturous threats. As the Lord walked to His end, He had every reason to feel embittered and indignant toward the human race. An inevitable and unrestrained crescendo of hostility was intent upon discharging all of its brutal violence onto Love, Himself.

What was Love's response? Unfathomable mercy. Jesus did not withdraw from the scene to seethe with resentment. While His cherished people, for whom He would willingly suffer a thousand deaths, were crushing Him with radical rejection, His pain was never centered on Himself. At no point during the Passion was Jesus wrapped up in His own experience, demanding recognition or an account from humanity. We never encounter Him rubbing salt into the wounds of His frustrations or relishing the bitter-sweet fruit of self-pity—as if there were no other reality in the world except His failure, or as if history ought to be judged on the sole basis of His own misfortune.

Even though He was the very eye of the storm, we see in the Gospels that He was entirely oblivious of self and forever reaching out to others. We were the reason for His suffering, and yet we were His sole concern.

Jesus had a careful word for His friend, turned traitor: *"Judas, are you betraying the Son of Man with a kiss?"* (Luke 22:48). He showed concern that His disciples should not suffer the same fate as He: *"If you are looking for me, let these men go"* (John 18:8). As He was being taken away to be slaughtered, He gently repaired the right ear of the high priest's servant (Luke 22:51). To Peter, tangled up in human weakness, He cast a saving glance (Luke 22:61). On the way to the Cross, He gave a heartfelt warning to the women who wept for Him (Luke 23:28). To the good thief, dying on the cross, He spoke the words every one of us longs to hear: *"Amen, I say to you, today you will be with me in Paradise"* (Luke 23:43). In the crucible of unfathomable agony, He offered a tender gesture of protection and filial devotion, leaving His mother in the care of His beloved disciple, John (John 19:25-27). And at the height of unspeakable physical pain and anguish of heart, Jesus worried most about His enemies: *"Father forgive them, they know not what they do"* (Luke 23:34).

Therefore, as imitators of the One Who lived among us and died for us, what reason do we have to refuse to love? And what excuse do we have for withholding mercy?

46th Star

AWE

(also called Fear of the
Lord – one of the seven
Gifts of the Holy Spirit)

Imagine heaven. Think of the most joyful moment that has graced your life, and magnify that by one billion. Still, that precious flash in time cannot compare to the smallest touches of paradise. Once there, you feel so blessedly peaceful and happy that all you can do is smile, all you can do is laugh. Imagine your every sadness erased, your every expectation exceeded, your every request answered, your every wish happening.

Jesus, Mary, and all of the saints who have gone before you are there—those you studied in life and others you are encountering for the very first time. Surrounding you in rapture are myriads of souls you have loved and who have loved you. Together with them and a cloud of angels and archangels, you fly through the eternal Kingdom admiring God's wonders, and you come to understand the jubilation of the Father in His work of creation.

Envision every good thing you've ever treasured available at your fingertips. Fancy every man, woman, child, and animal loving you dearly. Contemplate living healthy and happy for a million years. Imagine everything you taste dazzling your palate, everything you touch delighting your skin, everything you see leaving you intoxicated with awe. Ponder knowing everything and nothing but love. Disharmony with self, others, the world, is gone.

Picture life like that . . . then a million times greater than that, and you still cannot conceive of the magnitude of eternal glory. Visualize a never-ending multiplication of that, and you still cannot see the joys of paradise.

Each soul in heaven mirrors God's immeasurable love, and so when you and an inhabitant of heaven look upon each other, you are ravished by the Holy Spirit and lifted up in ecstasy even more. Just when you believe you have attained all the joy your soul could desire, the Father fills you with more. You become a dazzling light burning ever more brightly. You come to understand that this will never end. It will only grow, as the Father has an endless supply of love that He delights in sharing.

As you take hands with your companion saints and gaze upon the splendor of the Almighty, your spirit explodes like a firework of ecstasy. As the light from your spirit is caressed by those around you, every soul and spirit unite to become one with God, and then you feel what you never thought possible.

United within the beatific vision, one with the glorious Trinity, you feel all the love in eternity entering into you. You feel and see all the good things that have transpired since time began. You become part of it all and one with every loving thought or action shared across mankind and among angels. You melt into every breath of love there ever was, is, or will be. And then you understand what heaven truly is.[3]

---

[3] Adapted from the book *Messages to Carver Alan Ames* by C. Alan Ames.

"Listen, put it into your heart, my dearest one, that the thing that disturbs you, the thing that afflicts you, is nothing. Do not let your countenance, your heart be disturbed. Do not fear any sickness, nor anything that is sharp or hurtful. Am I not here, I, who am your Mother? Are you not under my shadow and protection? Am I not the source of your joy? Are you not in the hollow of my mantle, in the crossing of my arms? Do you need anything more?"

PRAYER OF CONSECRATION TO MARY

(for two or more persons. Turn the page for the single consecration.)

Pope John Paul II's Prayer to Our Lady of Guadalupe given in Mexico City, January 1979, while visiting Her basilica during his first foreign trip as Pope

"O Immaculate Virgin, Mother of the true God and Mother of the Church!, who from this place reveal your clemency and your pity to all those who ask for your protection, hear the prayer that we address to you with filial trust, and present it to your Son Jesus, our sole Redeemer.

Mother of Mercy, teacher of hidden and silent sacrifice, to you, who come to meet us sinners, we consecrate on this day all our being and all our love. We also consecrate to you our life, our work, our joys, our infirmities, and our sorrows. Grant peace, justice and prosperity to our people; for we entrust to your care all that we have and all that we are, our Lady and Mother. We wish to be entirely yours and to walk with you along the way of complete faithfulness to Jesus Christ in His Church. Hold us always with your loving hand.

Virgin of Guadalupe, Mother of the Americas, we pray to you for all the bishops, that they may lead the faithful along paths of intense Christian life, of love and humble service of God and souls. Contemplate this immense harvest, and intercede with the Lord that He may instill a hunger for holiness in the whole people of God, and grant abundant vocations of priests and religious, strong in the faith and zealous dispensers of God's mysteries.

Grant to our homes the grace of loving and respecting life in its beginnings, with the same love with which you conceived in your womb the life of the Son of God. Blessed Virgin Mary, protect our families, so that they may always be united, and bless the upbringing of our children.

Our hope, look upon us with compassion, teach us to go continually to Jesus and, if we fall, help us to rise again, to return to Him, by means of the confession of our faults and sins in the Sacrament of Penance, which gives peace to the soul.

We beg you to grant us a great love for all the holy Sacraments, which are, as it were, the signs that your Son left us on earth.

Thus, Most Holy Mother, with the peace of God in our conscience, with our hearts free from evil and hatred, we will be able to bring to all true joy and true peace, which come to us from your Son, our Lord Jesus Christ, who with God the Father and the Holy Spirit, lives and reigns for ever and ever. Amen."

PRAYER OF CONSECRATION TO MARY
(for one person)

"O Immaculate Virgin, Mother of the true God and Mother of the Church!, who from this place reveal your clemency and your pity to all those who ask for your protection, hear the prayer that I address to you with filial trust, and present it to your Son Jesus, our sole Redeemer.

Mother of Mercy, teacher of hidden and silent sacrifice, to you, who come to meet us sinners, I consecrate on this day all my being and all my love. I also consecrate to you my life, my work, my joys, my infirmities, and my sorrows. Grant peace, justice and prosperity to our people; for I entrust to your care all that I have and all that I am, my Lady and Mother. I wish to be entirely yours and to walk with you along the way of complete faithfulness to Jesus Christ in His Church. Hold me always with your loving hand.

Virgin of Guadalupe, Mother of the Americas, I pray to you for all the bishops, that they may lead the faithful along paths of intense Christian life, of love and humble service of God and souls. Contemplate this immense harvest, and intercede with the Lord that He may instill a hunger for holiness in the whole people of God, and grant abundant vocations of priests and religious, strong in the faith and zealous dispensers of God's mysteries.

Grant to my home the grace of loving and respecting life in its beginnings, with the same love with which you conceived in your womb the life of the Son of God. Blessed Virgin Mary, protect my family, so that they may always be united, and bless the upbringing of the children.

Our hope, look upon me with compassion, teach me to go continually to Jesus and, if I fall, help me to rise again, to return to Him, by means of the confession of my faults and sins in the Sacrament of Penance, which gives peace to the soul.

I beg you to grant me a great love for all the holy Sacraments, which are, as it were, the signs that your Son left us on earth.

Thus, Most Holy Mother, with the peace of God in my conscience, with my heart free from evil and hatred, I will be able to bring to all true joy and true peace, which come to me from your Son, our Lord Jesus Christ, who with God the Father and the Holy Spirit, lives and reigns for ever and ever. Amen."

CERTIFICATE OF CONSECRATION

This certificate is to verify that

_____

has made the act of

Total Consecration to Mary

on

_____

the feast of

_____

in accordance with Mary's Mantle Consecration

Mother of Mercy, teacher of hidden and silent sacrifice, to you, who come to meet us sinners, we consecrate on this day all our being and all our love. We also consecrate to you our life, our work, our joys, our infirmities and our sorrows. Grant peace, justice, and prosperity to our peoples; for we entrust to your care all that we have and all that we are, our Lady and Mother. We wish to be entirely yours and to walk with you along the way of complete faithfulness to Jesus Christ in His Church. Hold us always with your loving hand.

—St. Pope John Paul II

Certificates to sign for your consecration can be printed from the website page:
www.MarysMantleConsecration.com.

GOING FORWARD

BY MONSIGNOR JAMES MURPHY

My wish for you is that this Mary's Mantle Consecration will not be a one-time event but something life-altering, something that will change your prayer life permanently. That means not being afraid to do the 46-day spiritual retreat all over again, several times even (or another form of prayer that you find helpful). Spiritual directors tell us that true prayer is a way of life, not just something we resort to in cases of emergency. We need to make prayer a deeply rooted habit so that when the need arises, we are already in practice.

That means using your time properly, spending more of it in prayer and less of it doing nothing, or killing time. We use that phrase a lot—killing time—as if time was a nuisance that needed to be "killed," rather than a priceless opportunity to come closer to God. The time you have in this world is limited. Don't waste it.

However, this also means having determination. While all of us have a deep desire for a more intimate relationship with God, we also suffer from some ambivalence—conflicting desires, such as doubts or fears or hurts that come from the past. The way to handle these conflicts is with honesty, telling God about them and placing them at His feet. If you do that, you will be surprised at how fast the conflicts will evaporate and your intimacy with God will grow.

May you be protected by Mary's mantle as you walk this important road of prayer and live out the consecration you have just made.

A NOTE TO THE READER
AMAZON REVIEWS

If you enjoyed this consecration book, would you kindly post a short review of *Mary's Mantle Consecration: A Spiritual Retreat for Heaven's Help* on Amazon.com? Your support will make a difference in the lives of souls and help more people to grow spiritually and consecrate their lives to the Blessed Mother.

To leave a short review, go to Amazon.com and type in *Mary's Mantle Consecration*. Click on the book and scroll down the page. Next to customer reviews, click on "Write a customer review."

WOULD YOUR PARISH LIKE TO DO MARY'S MANTLE CONSECRATION?

IN THIS CRITICAL TIME IN THE CHURCH AND IN HUMAN HISTORY, ISN'T IT VITAL FOR CATHOLICS TO GROW IN VIRTUE, THE GIFTS OF THE HOLY SPIRIT, AND TO CONSECRATE THEIR LIVES TO THE BLESSED MOTHER?

Parishes around the nation are offering Mary's Mantle Consecration with great success and parishioners' gratitude. All it takes is a pastor's and a coordinator's yes.
See www.MarysMantleConsecration.com for details.

OTHER BOOKS
BY THE AUTHOR

Available through
QueenofPeaceMedia.com and Amazon.com in
Print, Ebook, and Audiobook formats

Libros disponible en español
www.queenofpeacemedia.com/libreria-catolica

EL AVISO
Testimonios y Profecías de la Iluminación de Conciencia

EL MANTO DE MARÍA
Una Consagración Mariana para Ayuda Celestial

EL MANTO DE MARÍA
Diario de Oración para la Consagración

TRANSFIGURADA
La Historia de Patricia Sandoval

HOMBRES JUNTO A MARÍA
Así Vencieron Seis Hombres la Más Ardua Batalla de Sus Vidas

THE WARNING

TESTIMONIES AND PROPHECIES OF
THE ILLUMINATION OF CONSCIENCE
with *IMPRIMATUR*

Endorsed by Bishop Gavin Ashenden, Msgr. Ralph J. Chieffo, Fr. John Struzzo, Mark Mallet, Fr. Berdardin Mugabo, and more…
Includes the fascinating story of Marino Restrepo, hailed as a St. Paul for our century

(See www.queenofpeacemedia.com/the-warning for the book trailer)

The Warning has been an Amazon #1 best-seller, ever since its release. In the book are authentic accounts of saints and mystics of the Church who have spoken of a day when we will all see our souls in the light of truth, and fascinating stories of those who have already experienced it for themselves.

"With His divine love, He will open the doors of hearts and illuminate all consciences. Every person will see himself in the burning fire of divine truth. It will be like a judgment in miniature."
—Our Lady to Fr. Stefano Gobbi of the Marian Movement of Priests

116

OF MEN AND MARY

HOW SIX MEN WON THE GREATEST BATTLE OF THEIR LIVES

"Of Men and Mary is superb. The six life testimonies contained within it are miraculous, heroic, and truly inspiring."

—Fr. Gary Thomas
Pastor, exorcist, and subject of the book and movie, "The Rite."

**(See www.queenofpeacemedia.com/of-men-and-mary
For the book trailer and to order)**

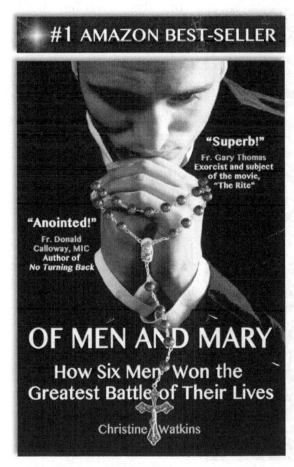

**"Anointed!"
—Fr. Donald Calloway,
MIC**

Turn these pages, and you will find yourself surprisingly inspired by a murderer locked up in prison, a drug-using football player who dreamed of the pros, and a selfish, womanizing dare-devil who died and met God. You will root for a husband and father whose marriage was a battleground, a man searching desperately to belong, pulled by lust and illicit attractions, and an innocent lamb who lost, in a single moment, everyone he cared about most. And you will rejoice that their sins and their pasts were no obstacle for heaven.

FULL OF GRACE

MIRACULOUS STORIES OF HEALING AND CONVERSION THROUGH MARY'S INTERCESSION

"Christine Watkins's beautiful and touching collection of conversion stories are direct, honest, heart-rending, and miraculous."
—**Wayne Weible**
Author of *Medjugorje: The Message*

(See www.queenofpeacemedia.com/full-of-grace for the book trailer and to order)

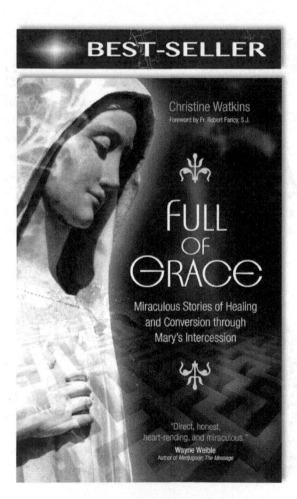

In this riveting book, Christine Watkins tells her dramatic story of miraculous healing and conversion to Catholicism, along with the stories of five others: a homeless drug addict, an altar boy trapped by cocaine, a stripper, a lonely youth, and a modern-day hero.

Following each story is a message that Mary has given to the world. And for those eager to probe the deeper, reflective waters of discipleship—either alone or within a prayer group—a Scripture passage, prayerful reflection questions, and a spiritual exercise at the end of each chapter offer an opportunity to enliven our faith.

TRANSFIGURED

PATRICIA SANDOVAL'S STORY

Endorsed by
**Archbishop Salvatore Cordileone & Bishop Michael C. Barber, SJ,
And Fr. Donald Calloway, MIC**

**Disponible También en Español: TRANSFIGURADA
avalado por EMMANUEL
(See www.queenofpeacemedia.com/transfigured
for the book trailer, the companion DVD, and to order)**

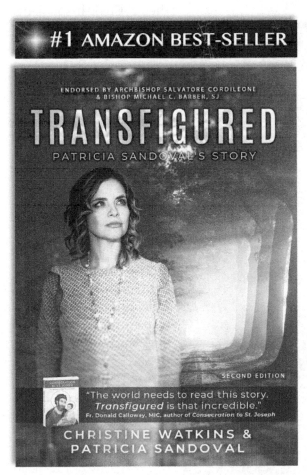

"Are you ready to read one of the most powerful conversion stories ever written? Seriously, are you? It's a bold and shocking claim, I admit. But the story you are about to have the pleasure of reading is so intense and brutally candid that I wouldn't be surprised if it brings you to tears multiple times and opens the door to an experience of mercy and healing. This story is made for the big screen, and I pray it makes it there someday. It's that incredible. . . What you are about to read is as raw, real, and riveting as a story can get. I couldn't put this book down!"

**—Fr. Donald
Calloway, MIC**
Author of
Consecration to St. Joseph and
No Turning Back

MARY'S MANTLE CONSECRATION

A SPIRITUAL RETREAT FOR HEAVEN'S HELP

Disponible también en español—*El Manto de María: Una Consagración Mariana para Ayuda Celestial*

Endorsed by **Archbishop Salvatore Cordileone** and **Bishop Myron J. Cotta**

(See www.MarysMantleConsecration.com to see a video of amazing testimonies and to order)

"I am grateful to Christine Watkins for making this disarmingly simple practice, which first grew in the fertile soil of Mexican piety, available to the English-speaking world."

—**Archbishop Salvatore Cordileone**

"Now more than ever, we need a miracle. Christine Watkins leads us through a 46-day self-guided retreat that focuses on daily praying of the Rosary, a Little fasting, and meditating on various virtues and the seven gifts of the Holy Spirit, leading to a transformation in our lives and in the people on the journey with us!"

—**Fr. Sean O. Sheridan, TOR**
Former President, Franciscan University of Steubenville

MARY'S MANTLE CONSECRATION

PRAYER JOURNAL
to accompany the consecration book

Disponible también en español—
El Manto de María: Diario de Oración para la Consagración

PREPARE FOR AN OUTPOURING
OF GRACE UPON YOUR LIFE

**(See www.MarysMantleConsecration.com
to see a video of amazing testimonies and to order)**

St. Pope John Paul II said that his consecration to Mary was "a decisive turning point in my life." It can be the same for you.

This *Prayer Journal* with daily Scriptures, saint quotes, questions for reflection and space for journaling is a companion book to the popular *Mary's Mantle Consecration*, a self-guided retreat that has resulted in miracles in the lives and hearts of those who have applied themselves to it. This prayer journal will take you even deeper into your soul and into God's transforming grace.

WINNING THE BATTLE FOR YOUR SOUL

JESUS' TEACHINGS THROUGH MARINO RESTREPO, A ST. PAUL FOR OUR CENTURY

Endorsed by Archbishop-Emeritus, Ramón C. Argüelles
"This book is an authentic jewel of God!"
—Internationally renowned author, María Vallejo-Nájera

(See <u>The Warning: Testimonies and Prophecies of the Illumination of Conscience</u> to read Marino's testimony)

Marino Restrepo was a sinful man kidnapped for ransom by Colombian terrorists and dragged into the heart of the Amazon jungle. In the span of just one night, the Lord gave him an illumination of his conscience followed by an extraordinary infusion of divine knowledge. Today, Marino is hailed as one of the greatest evangelizers of our time.

In addition to giving talks around the world, Marino is the founder of the Church-approved apostolate, Pilgrims of Love.

This book contains some of the most extraordinary teachings that Jesus has given to the world through Marino Restrepo, teachings that will profoundly alter and inform the way you see your ancestry, your past, your purpose, and your future.

122

IN LOVE WITH TRUE LOVE

THE UNFORGETTABLE STORY OF SISTER NICOLINA

(See www.QueenofPeaceMedia.com and Amazon.com)

In this seemingly loveless world of ours, we might wonder if true love is attainable. Is it real, or is it perhaps a dancing illusion captured on Hollywood screens? And if this love dares to exist, does it satisfy as the poets say, or fade in our hearing like a passing whisper?

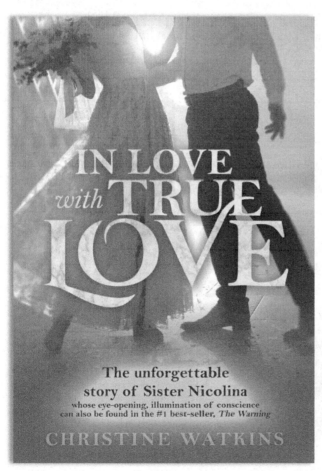

The souls are few who have discovered these answers, and one of them is Nicolina, a feisty, flirtatious girl who fell in love with the most romantic man in all of post-war Germany.

Little did they imagine the places where love would take them.

This enthralling real-life story is a glimpse into the grand secrets of true love—secrets that remain a conundrum to most, but are life, itself for a chosen few. Little-known chambers within the Heart of Love lie in hope to be discovered, and through this little book, may you, like Nicolina, enter their mystery and find life, too.

SHE WHO SHOWS THE WAY

HEAVEN'S MESSAGES
FOR OUR TURBULENT TIMES

"This book should be widely disseminated, all for God's glory and in honor of the Mother of God, for all of us and the holiness of Christ's disciples."
— **Ramón C. Argüelles, STL, Archbishop-Emeritus**
(See www.QueenofPeaceMedia.com and Amazon.com)

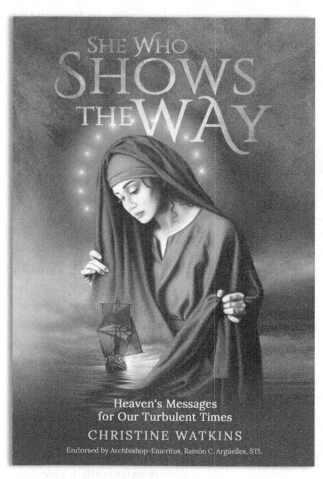

Our Mother knows when we most need her, and we need her now.

We are living in the end times, not the end of the world, but the end of an age. Those who wish to remain faithful to the Gospel are seeking heaven's guidance in order to weather and safely navigate the unparalleled storms ahead.

In this extraordinary and anointed book of messages from Mother Mary—and occasionally from Jesus— through inner-locutions to one of her most unlikely children, she has responded.

"A great turning point in the fate of your nation and its faith in God will soon be upon you, and I ask you all to pray and offer your sufferings for this cause. . ."
— **Our Lady's message of August 4, 1993**

MARIE-JULIE JAHENNY

PROPHECIES AND PROTECTION
FOR THE END TIMES

(See www.QueenofPeaceMedia.com. Soon on Amazon.com)

Marie-Julie Jahenny (1850-1941) is one of the most extraordinary mystics in the history of the Church. This humble peasant from devout parents in Britanny, France, received numerous visitations from heaven and lived

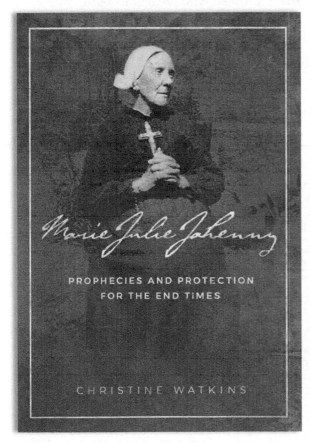

with multiple wounds of the stigmata for most of her long life. Jahenny's selfless spirit endures as a gift to the Church, for she received knowledge of what lies on the horizon of our current era.

Jahenny was supported by her local bishop, Msgr. Fournier of Nantes, who said of her, "I see nothing but good."

In addition to Jahenny's special mission from the Lord to spread the love of the Cross, she was called to prepare the world for the coming chastisements, which precede and prepare the world for the glorious renewal of Christendom in the promised era of peace.

Through Marie-Julie, the Lord has given help, remedies, and protection for the times we now live in, and those soon to come. As Christ said to her on several occasions, "I want My people to be warned."

PURPLE SCAPULAR

OF BLESSING AND PROTECTION
FOR THE END TIMES

Jesus and Mary have given this scapular to the world for our times!

Go to **www.queenofpeacemedia.com/product/purple-scapular-of-blessing-and-protection** to read about all of the incredible promises given to those who wear it in faith.

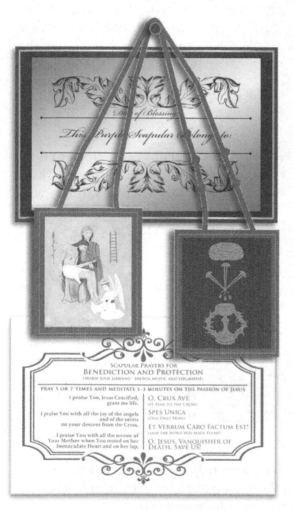

Our Lady's words to the mystic, stigmatist, and victim soul, Marie-Julie Jahenny: "My children, all souls, all people who possesses this scapular will see their family protected. Their home will also be protected, **foremost from fires**. . . for a long time my Son and I have had the desire to make known this scapular of benediction…

This first apparition of this scapular will be a new protection for the times of the chastisements, of the calamities, and the famines. All those who are clothed (with it) shall pass under the storms, the tempests, and the darkness. They will have light as if it were plain day. Such is the power of this unknown scapular. . ."

THE CROSS OF FORGIVENESS

FOR THE END TIMES

On July 20, 1882, Our Lord introduced **THE CROSS OF FORGIVENESS** to the world through the French mystic, Marie-Julie Jahenny. He indicated that He would like it made and worn by the faithful during the time of the chastisements. It is a cross signifying pardon, salvation, protection, and the calming of plagues.

Go to **www.queenofpeacemedia.com/product/cross-of-forgiveness** to read about all of the graces and protection given to those who wear it in faith.

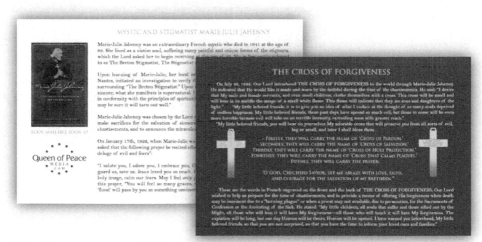

This bronze cross (1¾ inches tall and 1 inch wide) is a gift for our age and a future time when priests may not be readily available: "My little beloved friends, you will bear on yourselves My adorable cross that will preserve you from all sorts of evil, big or small, and later I shall bless them. . . My little children, all souls that suffer, and those sifted out by the blight, all those who will kiss it will have My forgiveness—all those who will touch it will have My forgiveness." The expiation will be long, but one day Heaven will be theirs, Heaven will be opened."

127

THE FLAME OF LOVE
THE SPIRITUAL DIARY
OF ELIZABETH KINDELMANN

(Go to www.QueenofPeaceMedia.com/flame-love-love-book-bundle) to receive the Flame of Love book bundle at cost!

Extraordinary graces of literally blinding Satan, and reaching heaven quickly are attached to the spiritual practices and promises in this spiritual classic. On August 2, 1962, Our Lady said these remarkable words to mystic and victim soul, Elizabeth Kindelmann:

"Since the Word became Flesh, I have never given such a great movement as the Flame of Love that comes to you now. Until now, there has been nothing that so blinds Satan."

ABOUT THE AUTHOR

Christine Watkins is a popular Catholic author and keynote speaker. She was an anti-Catholic atheist about to die from her sins when she received a divine healing. Watkins brings to life stories of faith, including her own, and fascinating topics of Catholic spirituality. See www.ChristineWatkins.com.

THE FLAME OF LOVE

In this special talk, Christine Watkins introduces the Flame of Love of the Immaculate Heart of Mary.

This worldwide movement in the Catholic Church is making true disciples of Jesus Christ in our turbulent times and preparing souls for the Triumph of Our Lady's Heart and the New Pentecost. Email cwatkins@queenofpeacemedia.com. See www.ChristineWatkins.com.

FIND YOUR WAY HOME

In this day-long retreat or 3-day parish mission, popular speakers, Fr. Rick Wendell and Christine Watkins, share their remarkable conversion stories (found in the books, *Of Men and Mary* plus *The Warning*, and *Full of Grace*, respectively), and explore 5 key steps to heaven: Eucharist, Reconciliation, Prayer, Fasting, and Bible Reading. Email cwatkins@queenofpeacemedia.com; see www.ChristineWatkins.com.

Made in the USA
Middletown, DE
26 October 2021